Sacred Fire

The Power of the First Element to Change Your Life

Maril Crabtree, author of *Sacred Feathers*, *Sacred Stones*, and *Sacred Waters*

Adams Media
Avon, Massachusetts

Published by Adams Media, an F+W Publications Company
57 Littlefield Street
Avon, MA 02322
www.adamsmedia.com

ISBN: 1-59337-366-X

Printed in Canada.
J I H G F E D C B A

Library of Congress Cataloging-in-Publication Data

Crabtree, Maril.
Sacred fire / Maril Crabtree.
p. cm.
ISBN 1-59337-366-X
1. Fire--Religious aspects--Meditations. I. Title.

BL453.C73 2005
202'.12--dc22

2005021883

This publication is designed to provide accurate and authoritative
information with regard to the subject matter covered. It is sold
with the understanding that the publisher is not engaged in
rendering legal, accounting, or other professional advice. If legal
advice or other expert assistance is required, the services of a
competent professional person should be sought.
—From a *Declaration of Principles* jointly adopted by a
Committee of the American Bar Association and
a Committee of Publishers and Associations

Interior photos © www.istockphoto.com.

This book is available at quantity discounts for bulk purchases.
For information, please call 1-800-872-5627.

To all those who know themselves as

divine sparks of sacred fire

and to those who keep the sacred fire

burning in my soul

CREDITS

CONTENTS

Part III

FIRE LEGACIES:

Stories of Fire from Other Lands, Other Times

Part IV

THE MYSTERY OF FIRE

Acknowledgments

I would like to acknowledge my wonderful writing friends, who not only supported me through the process of putting this book together, but who also listened patiently to my complaints along the way.

I acknowledge my editor, Kate Epstein, a superb advocate and talented editor, and all the members of the Adams Media staff who put care and attention into their work on my behalf.

A few people deserve acknowledgement for going "above and beyond" in their support and assistance: Deborah Shouse, a steadfast friend and constant source of inspiration; Bill Grover, whose eye for detail is invaluable; and Jim Crabtree, without whom I simply could not follow my heart's desires.

I acknowledge with gratitude the storytellers and poets who generously contributed their words to this book.

Finally, I acknowledge my readers, those kindred spirits who see the world through more than physical eyes. It is you I write for and you who inspire me.

INTRODUCTION

O! For a muse of fire, that would ascend the brightest heaven of invention.

.. . William Shakespeare, *Henry V*

Of the four great elements of nature—air, earth, water, and fire—fire seems the most mutable, taking a thousand forms and shapes, spawning hundreds of legends, reaching across time and space. There is the fire of sunlight, our source of life, and of starlight, a source of beauty and the earliest tool of navigation. The fire of candles, ancient sources of illumination, extended humanity's reach beyond the darkness. The fire of burning wood offered a source of warmth, comfort, and cooked food.

Fire permeates our lives and spiritual traditions. The fire of passion, ranging from the romantic allure of Eros to the passion for ideas, ravishes us. The birth canal's ring of fire ushers us into this world, and in many cultures the fire of a funeral pyre or cremation consumes our physical bodies at death. The cleansing fire and smoke of the Native American sweat lodge renews our spirits. The yogic tradition teaches the breath of fire and reveres kundalini, symbolized by the fiery snake that sits at the bottom of the spine.

Gods and goddesses of fire connect us to stories of burning bushes, flaming volcanoes, bonfires, and flickering lights. We savor the fiery imagination of the writer, the philosopher, the artist, the dreamer—what the ancient Celts referred to as "fire in the head."

Fire is also dangerous and is something we fear. Fire can wipe out our homes, our land, and our families. It can sweep through a thousand acres of prime development or a thousand acres of virgin timber without discrimination. Its capacity to destroy as well as to create life makes it the most potent natural element in many spiritual traditions.

Yet even in its destruction fire can bring gifts of renewal to the discerning eye and gifts of wisdom to the discerning soul. Those who experience fire know how it can melt powerful metals and, from that melting, forge new creations of strength and beauty.

In this book, you will find amazing and heartwarming and, yes, passionate stories that speak of how fire in many forms has burned its way into our lives. From fiery love stories to stories of forest fires to stories of firewalking, campfires, Olympic torches, candlelight rituals, and volcanic miracles—the element of fire speaks to the soul and has much to tell. It speaks sometimes in a whisper, sometimes in a roar, and has even been known to speak in tongues of flame. We need only to listen, to receive its magic and mystery, to allow ourselves to see the many gifts of fire and be transformed by them.

PART I
The Power of Fire

Stories of Healing and Empowerment

A Sacred Glow

Maril Crabtree

I was in Paris when I received news that my friend had died of the cancer she fought for three years. I felt sad and isolated. How could I honor her life and all that she and I had shared? I wanted to feel connected, although I was thousands of miles away from our mutual friends and her family.

The next morning I made my way across bridges and busy streets to L'Isle St. Louis, where the Cathedral of Notre Dame has witnessed countless births and deaths through the centuries. Approaching its massive carved doors, I slipped in among chattering tourist groups. My eyes feasted on carved statues of saints, intricate stained-glass windows, and ornate altar furnishings. I soaked up the smells of polished wood and brass, of burning candles. I ran my hands over the old pews and traced with my fingers the rough stone walls. Then I walked slowly to the flickering rows of candles, some lit and some still dark. Here, my tears could flow freely.

Always, candles are burning in these sacred places. The lights of dozens, sometimes hundreds, of votives twinkle and glow. Each candle represents the prayer of someone for someone else, living or dead, religious or not. I looked at the tiny flames nodding above their glass containers and thought of the souls who might hover here. Perhaps they listen to the heartfelt prayers and watch those who pause in the dim candlelight to give thanks for a world apart from the world they usually live in.

I thought of how the light from burning candles casts a holy glow in temples, mosques, synagogues, churches, monasteries, fields, and other places where people gather to reflect and pray. My friend and I had lit candles at outdoor peace vigils and at gatherings to pray for those caught in wars not of their own making. We sang in candlelight to mark the winter solstice, the rebirth of the sun.

With the taper that is always there for that purpose, I lit a single candle for my friend as I said my prayer, remembering our many years of friendship, picturing her wild hair, her startling eyes, her generous smile.

As I watched the tiny flame lighting the space around it, I affirmed the light she had given, and would continue to give, to me and to others. I stepped back, taking in all of the candles, seeing that my prayer had joined with others, envisioning a symphony of souls being prayed for.

No matter where I am on my travels, I try to enter a sacred place and light a candle—for each of us, for all of us. I light a candle for the person who is ill and perhaps dying; for those who feel desperate and hopeless; for the lonely, the lost, the homeless. Candles throw their light into the darkness, and in so doing they give us access to hope and a deep sense of connection with ourselves, with each other, and with the mystery that enfolds us.

I take comfort in knowing that the candles will continue to burn long after I leave the sanctuary, just as our prayers, spoken and unspoken, continue to light the way for each other.

A Gift of Fire

Anna Buckner

"Is this me?" I asked the wind, sitting on a pile of ashes, half-burned papers, and smoldering stuffed animals. "Is there a purpose to this nightmare?"

The fire spread rapidly. My mother and I were in the kitchen when we saw smoke rising above the doorway. We rushed to the corridor. Already the heat was oppressive. At the far end of the hallway, my bedroom was shooting flames out the door. We barely had time to run out of the apartment.

Kind neighbors opened their doors and we called the fire station. Mountains of snow prevented traffic from moving fast. It took the firefighters half an hour to get to our building. By then, the damage was done. Nevertheless, we were alive, although shocked.

When we re-entered the apartment, the smell was terrible. Inside the kitchen cabinets, the Tupperware had melted into globs of white plastic. Some of them had melted over the edge of the shelf and onto the shelf underneath, weaving a cobweb of plastic threads linking shelf to shelf.

My bedroom was empty and dark as a cave. Whatever was not burned had been thrown outside onto the sidewalk. A pile of smoldering ashes. Childhood memories, secret diaries, schoolbooks, research for my next paper. All gone. My clothes. My guitar. My bed.

There's something eerie about picking out remnants of your life from the sidewalk. I remember a fierce wind when I went out to look at the pile. Snow covered the top half of my old life. Smoke still escaped from the inside of the mound. Several half-burned pieces of paper gently glided away in the sky, like feathers on the wind.

You don't think about not being materialistic when something like this happens. You want your things back. Now. You want your life back, the way it was before.

But did I really want it back?

For years, had I not made loud noises about leaving for a foreign country? Had I not made half-baked plans several times to go out on my own? Had I not dreamed of being far away from here?

I stayed long enough to help my mother redo the apartment and get settled again. Friends came by to offer shelter and help scrub furniture.

Then, I boarded a plane for England.

For a year, I thought back on the fire. The fire that wrecked my sleepy life. The fire that made me move. The fire that kicked me out of torpor and into action, from dream to reality. Not just a fire. A cosmic wake-up call. An alarm clock set by the Powers That Be. A gift of fire.

There is also a mystery attached to this blaze. The firefighters never found an explanation for its start. The captain shrugged and said something about a "possible bad plug." Yet the electricity had been checked recently and the insurance agent did not think there was a problem there.

To this day, seventeen years later, there is no explanation.

But I know what it was. I know this fire was for me. How else can I account for the fact that only my bedroom was reduced to ashes?

I know it was sent as a present to open up a new life. It was a sacred fire, a liberating fire, a purifying fire. A sacred fire needed to instill life in the corpse-like Frankenstein I had become. A fire of hope. And it was not too big or powerful. Just enough to get me started on the right path.

Today, when I see a fire in a fireplace, I am not scared. I think "thank you." Thank you for having been the agent of my freedom. For making space for the new. New clothes, new guitar, new bed, and, most importantly, a new and happy life.

Initiation by Fire

Julie Biro

*T*wo weeks into the new millennium, we were having one of our very hot summers with temperatures more than 100 degrees, and it hadn't rained for a while. Summer for me was a mixed blessing. It brought the hot weather that I love but also a reminder of the potential risk of fire. I live in a bushfire-prone area in the foothills of the Dandenong Mountain Ranges, near Melbourne, Australia.

I awoke in the middle of the night to the smell of smoke. I was immediately on alert, my mind racing with many thoughts. Where's the fire? How will I see it in the dark? How will I know what direction it's coming from? How long has it been burning? What do I need to do? Should I wake my husband, Laci? Should I ring the fire brigade? I started to panic. My heart beat fast and I sat up in bed staring out at the mountain range across the road, looking for evidence. I was just about to get out of bed and wake Laci, when my inner voice said clearly, *It's all right. There's no fire now but there will be tomorrow. Don't worry, you will all be safe and so will your home.*

My head sank back in the pillows and the panic of moments ago vanished in a warm, fuzzy haze of peace and comfort. It filled my body and mind and sent me straight back to sleep.

The next day, Laci and I went to work at our studio two streets away. We set about loading the kilns with the glass bowls, plates, and platters we make to earn our living. By lunchtime, it was 105 degrees. Normally, we would keep working despite the heat. We had a certain volume of stock to produce each week, but this day we decided to go home. When we arrived, we closed up the house, drew the blinds, and turned on ceiling fans to keep the heat out. Our miniature black poodles, Peter and Tara, and our fluffy black cat, Thira, were happy to lie under the fans.

I decided to do a load of washing because the clothes would be dry in no time. As I was hanging them on the line, I noticed a large column of smoke rising out of gum trees across the other side of the main road, on the street diagonally opposite ours. It didn't register at first. I thought it must be someone burning off a field. That made no sense, as there was a total ban on fires that day.

Then I saw the police helicopter and the orange light plane, equipped with water bomber, dropping water on the fire. Soon local news choppers arrived and circled low around us and over the fire. Suddenly, I remembered the message I'd been given the night before. I was amazed I'd forgotten it until now.

"Laci, there's a fire close by. Don't worry. I was awakened last night and told we would be safe."

His response was to put our emergency fire plan into action. I followed him outside to help and he began hosing down the house and the gravel paths around it. Sirens were blaring as police and fire trucks roared down the main road. Soon thick smoke was billowing up the street. Police had blocked off the road at both ends. Occasionally, cars tore up the road, the drivers looking frightened. They had obviously been allowed to go through to check on their homes and animals.

9

I walked further down the main road and saw that another fire had sprung up close to it. Firefighters were hosing it down. The whole experience was surreal. Usually I'd be in a state of severe anxiety by now, but I was calm. My senses felt heightened as if I were in an altered state of consciousness.

I did all the things I'd been told not to do in a situation like this. The fire management plan adopted by our shire advises us to stay on our property to watch for sparks and embers from the fire front so they can be quickly put out. I was a lone observer standing by the side of the main road, watching the drama unfold around me.

We are advised to wear clothes of a natural material that will cover as much as possible to protect from radiant heat, as the fire gets closer. I was standing there wearing a light sleeveless dress and sandals. It was strange to know that my curiosity wasn't foolhardy, as I'd had reassurance from my inner voice that I would be safe.

I came back inside to give Laci an update. He had the TV on and our fire was headline news. According to the news reports, the whole of our suburb was ablaze. I looked at Laci.

"Imagine if we weren't home and saw the news, we'd be beside ourselves. Think of all the people who live around here and can't get past the roadblocks. What must they be thinking? What they're saying isn't true at all." He agreed.

I alternated between watching TV and going outside to see if the fire was abating or getting any closer. There was no fear, only fascination. The smoke started to ease, and by late afternoon a wind change pushed the fire away from us. By teatime, it was well under control.

The main road had reopened and a weak cool change brought a little bit of rain. The news continued to show the old footage of the fire still blazing out of control, maintaining the hype and fear.

I was in an altered state until late that night. I wanted to stay in this space of trust, flow, and detachment indefinitely. It felt so good.

Imagine what it would be like living like this all the time, I kept thinking to myself.

Finally, we went to bed. I lay and looked out the window, too excited to sleep. I could hear thunder in the distance, and lightning flashes lit our room. I hadn't been keen on thunderstorms since a lightning bolt came through the kitchen window when I was a child. I was comforted by the trust that had been built in me from the day's events, so I decided to let go and enjoy the storm.

The next moment a blinding flash of white light, similar to descriptions I've read from people who have witnessed a vision of Jesus or Mary, lit the room, forcing me to shield my eyes from its brilliance. Next came an almighty crack that woke Laci.

"Oh, God. It will start another fire. Go out and look," I yelled.

You didn't warn me about this one, I called out loud to my higher self. Laci went to turn on the front light but the power was out. He grabbed the flashlight from the kitchen.

"Are the power lines down or was it just lightning?"

"I can't see anything, it's too dark." It was raining heavily by now. I was shaking as Laci came in and closed the door.

At first light, I went outside to have a look after a restless night's sleep. I found a huge branch of a gum tree had fallen across our car and damaged the hood. It was still drivable. None of the power lines was down, so the lightning must have struck the tree, causing it to make that awful cracking sound.

That year we had the worst bushfires in Australia in nearly seventy years. It felt like the whole of Australia was ablaze. Some parts of the country hadn't had rain in months. Water restrictions were in force because the reservoirs were so low.

I was on alert, but not like before the millennium fire. Such was my trust in my higher self now, Laci and I decided to go away to the coast for a few days. Normally, we didn't leave in the fire danger period.

Our friends came to look after the house and the animals. We drove off on yet another day of total fire ban, the temperature 105 degrees. I was a little anxious leaving but my inner voice whispered, *There will be a little fire close to home, but it's nothing to worry about; it's safe to go away.*

That night from our motel room, we watched an apocalyptic sunset as smoke from fires that had broken out where we passed earlier that day swirled through the clouds and obscured the sun.

I rang my friends to tell them where we were staying, and they didn't mention there had been any fires at home. Nor did the news reports. Other fires broke out across the state. We followed the smoke home.

Our friends were quick to tell us when we got home that there had been a grass fire across the road. They had watched it from the front veranda and it had been put out quickly.

My initiation by fire allowed me to live from the perspective of my wiser self that sees the bigger picture of my life and lives it without fear. It gave me a tangible experience of how that self helps me navigate my way through the fear that is only part of the human reality. It reassured me that I was always protected, even if I was in danger. I am strengthened by this initiation and feel more whole. It gives me the courage to move forward in my life every day.

Carrying Fire in My Soul

Leslie Howard Antley

I was not, by nature, an outgoing or athletic person. But when Shell Oil Company sponsored the 1986 Olympic Festival, I was among those who carried the torch.

At first, all I did was accompany the torchbearer walking around the Woodcreek facility that morning before daybreak. Up and down hills, over the creek, and among the trees we meandered, circling the facility before handing off the torch to others who would do the same at the Conoco facility next door. Never deviating from the path set before me, I never suspected the ways in which my life was about to change.

Later that morning, I boarded a bus that drove us to Memorial Park in the center of Houston. While we all wore the requisite T-shirts emblazoned with the modern-style scallop-shell emblem to declare our affiliation with the oil and gas community, others were dressed in typical runner's clothing . . . short shorts, running shoes, and duck-billed gimme caps. Firm bodies with sleek muscles, they all appeared to know exactly where they were going in life and what they were going to do to get there. I was still pretty clueless about my goals in life, even at age twenty-eight.

Aware that I didn't compare favorably to the others, I wore blue jeans with my Shell T-shirt. Instead of the gimme cap, it was my dad's hardhat with the pre-1980s logo on the front. As a second-generation employee, I needed to keep faith with the old as well as the new.

Finally, in the heart of the park, it was my turn to run the gauntlet of cheering Houstonians. As the torch passed to me, my first impression was how heavy it was, yet how cool the handle felt. I started running, peripherally aware of voices in the distance yelling, "She's wearing a hardhat!" and "Go, girl!"

The world seemed to come to a stop . . . even as traffic had been halted to allow runners the right-of-way. Or was it a rite-of-way in my life? As my feet slapped the pavement, the roaring sound of the fire being consumed in the torch mesmerized me. Its song seemed to burn away my insecurities, purifying my purpose in life. It was a public declaration to the world that no matter what had or would happen to me in life, I was determined to endure. Not only endure, but triumph.

After what seemed an eternity, I passed the torch to the next sleek runner. My arms ached with relief as complete strangers pounded me on the back and shoulders, congratulating me for completing my portion in the torch run. In a daze, I returned to the office, bemused by my accomplishment.

Days stretched into months, months into years. Amid the unrelenting bustle of work and family, despair tried many times to overtake me, to extinguish me. The fire that had sustained me became banked coals, barely warm in the ashes of my life.

❧

Returning to the university in the fall of 2001, tiny flickers began to appear once more. As I regained my confidence, I came to realize that the fire had always been just under the surface, waiting to blaze forth through the darkness of my life. From that moment on, each time I saw a candle lit my soul quivered with remembrance of that morning in Houston when the torch I carried was the fire in my soul, visible for the world to see.

Olympic Flame

James Penha

Swathed in sweat, stars and crescents,
I sing my soul's epic
race
to a coliseum fired
by my naked
freedom.

A Shoe Burning

Candace Carrabus

"The shoes burn at sunset," I announced. "At the top of the hill in the field by the pond."

A bemused smile creased my husband's face. Of all the questions he might venture about this peculiar statement, he asked, "Why sunset?"

I had given this some thought. It was dead of winter, and night came early. "The wind settles then," I said. "Plus, I want my offering to be visible to whatever gods note such things."

Ever one to add an artistic touch, Robert fashioned a torch for me to safely light the pyre I had built, and he readied enough gasoline to ensure a good blaze.

"It's a hell of a way to mark your fortieth," he said.

I had decided to burn the shoes some months before. I wanted a ritual to celebrate turning forty. Setting fire to something from my past felt like the perfect transition from the frivolous pursuits of youth to the more pertinent matters of maturity—from heels and skirts to flats and slacks. For it was not any pair of worn-out footwear I intended to immolate, but the strappy black snakeskin high heels with tiny gold buckles that fastened around my ankles. When I was still willing to forgo comfort in the name of fashion, these shoes had seen a good deal of wear. My knees and back thanked me daily for giving up such foolishness.

The old me would go up in smoke and the new, wiser me would emerge from the ashes shod in comfortable loafers—or in the case of a cold and snowy winter's day—practical mukluks. Never again would I bend to someone else's idea of who I should be. In the future, I would be true to myself.

My fortieth birthday dawned clear and icy— common enough for January in the Midwest. Our farm straddles a ridge where wind slices across as if nothing stands between us and the North Pole but a couple of barbed wire fences. Undaunted, I built a column of glued-together cardboard boxes and affixed the sacrificial shoes on top like an overwrought cake decoration.

When the appointed time arrived, we bundled into our insulated coveralls and fur-lined hats and marched into the waning winter light, me carrying the tower reverently like the offering it was, Robert following with torch and tinder. Our black lab and six cats with tails held high completed the procession, but made for home when ice hardened between their toes.

At the top of the hill in the field by the pond, steady blasts of air had scoured the snow to a smooth, crisp finish that glowed softly with the muted violet and red of a dusky winter sunset. I met the western sky with eager eyes, seeing not the end of my youth, but the beginning of a future filled with promise.

I put down my gift and took a moment to admire the whole of it. The brown and tan boxes rose in mismatched symmetry from large to small, and here and there, gobs of glue dripped over an edge. My homemade altar was sturdy, not pretty, yet the shoes looked ready to step away. Part of me hated to lose them. Those spiky, impractical bits of leather appeared insubstantial, especially against a bitter January night, but they held memories of going places, of conversations without end, of dancing.

You must be willing to give something up, I told myself, and there is so much to gain. The shoes are a symbol. You do not want high heels on the path you now walk, nor do you need them to talk all night, or to dance.

The frigid breeze biting my cheek reminded me to move. Robert lit the torch; I held it to a lower box. We stood back and watched as flames coursed upward. The fire burned hot and fast, melting the shoes from view quicker than expected, spiraling cinders into the purple sky. Heat seared through me and thawed a circle in the snow. Moved by the spirit of the moment, and perhaps to prove my point about dancing, I giddily spun around the blaze, waving the torch while my husband snapped photos.

During the jog back to our house, new buoyancy lifted my steps, as if I had crossed an invisible threshold from a weighted past to a lighter future.

Six years later, that fire still warms my inner world. Cleansed of old, restrictive thoughts, I go forward unrestrained, often barefoot. And somewhere at the top of the hill in the field by the pond, or in a nest or burrow nearby, two tiny gold buckles remember, and glitter like miniature flames.

Interior Decorating

Rev. Karen Coussens

As a child of the '50s and '60s, homemaking was a large part of my education. I learned and accepted that the husband goes out into the world and "brings home the bacon" while the wife stays in and "keeps the home fires burning." The home fires, yes—the stove, the fireplace, the furnace . . . but never the candles.

Candles, I learned in my Interior Decorating My Home class, were decorative items. Burning candles caused smoke and soot, melting them out of their pretty shapes with a piece of blackened wick leaning out of their tops. Oh, the mess from the blobs of melted wax oozing onto tables and shelves! In the home where "neatness counts," candles remained in decorative holders, unlit.

As a young housewife, I attended candle parties and demonstrations. I had lovely matching or accenting candles in each room, and centerpieces with candles in or around them on holiday or special event tables. Of course, I also kept emergency candles that could be lit if the power went out, but one hoped that flashlights would make that unnecessary.

After twenty-six years of marriage and homemaking, my children had left to keep their own homes. The candles were still decorative and unlit. Then one November, my husband died suddenly of a heart attack, and home became as cold as those unlit candles. Interior decorating was meaningless to me. My own "interior" became empty and bleak.

I struggled for two years to accept this drastic change in my life. I had counseling, I read every book on grief that I found in libraries or stores. I became a decorative item. I still looked good, made a nice addition to places I was put, and decorated holiday tables as before. There was no burning, though, no smoke, soot, or unwelcome globs of fallout from my presence. In grief as in life, neatness counted.

Some of the books I read suggested that burning a candle on the anniversary of the birth or death of a loved one was an accepted way of honoring them. On the third anniversary of my husband's death, still trying to find some way to come to terms with it, I decided to light a candle.

Arising early (sleep still was not a comfortable time), I found a white vanilla-scented pillar candle. With tears falling freely, I lit it with reverence and with words of love, honoring my husband and his influence on my life. I watched as the light filled the small room. Shadows moved along the walls and ceilings, swaying as if dancing. Suddenly, I remembered the dances we shared, the times of fun singing around a campfire, the romantic fires in the fireplace at home on chilly evenings after the children were in bed. To my surprise, the tears turned to smiles and the reflection of the candle's flickering light began to warm and decorate an interior place within me.

Not only was I much like the candle; love, I realized, was like the candle, too. We can be beautiful in appearance, shown to advantage by an external, loving light, and serve a purpose that brings warmth and light to our surroundings. There is the truth of light and shadow within us, and the ability to brighten and warm spaces. There are times when an external light is sufficient to show us to our best advantage, and there is sometimes a great need for us to recognize and shine our own light. Most important is to know that the power of our light is available at all times.

I have moved into a new home. It is decorated simply, with many windows bringing in the beauty of nature. There are many candles around, beautiful candles in lovely holders—every one of them with a glob of wax that falls naturally down its side and adds dimension to the form as its light shines. The wicks are dark and many of them lean to the side, as if reaching for the next flame to touch them and give them life. "Keeping the home fires burning" has a new meaning: letting my own fire decorate my interior.

A Rite of Spring

Dru Clarke

So, like a forgotten fire, a childhood can always flare up again within us.

... Gaston Bachelard

pril's lengthening days are an attractive nuisance. While my husband and I should be working on tax returns and attending to annual spring housecleaning, the yellow light, sapphire skies, and the greening up of the earth's skin are too much to resist. They bring out the kid in us.

We break out the drip torches or the matches, the rakes, wet towels or water carts, the drag line behind the pickup—depending on how sophisticated our approach—and head for the pastures and twiggy wood lots with their limb and leaf litter. We mow the property edge close to the fence lines. We bundle up in protective gear, cover our skin, wear thick-soled shoes. We test the wind with a wet finger, assess the relative humidity, alert the county. It is time to burn.

Long before I moved to the Flint Hills, I flew over Kansas one spring night—it must have been April—and sections of it glowed like a phosphorescent sea. Back east, such a sight would have generated panic and finger-wagging scolding: how can you DO such a thing? Think of the air pollution, think of the poor animals. Talk about a shift of paradigms: fire and its complement, grazing, are GOOD for this land.

It begins this way. The first bunch of grass sparks, sputters, then bursts into flame. One match to combust this patch. How deft will I have to be to raze the entire north pasture? I work my leaf rake and pull glowing leaves and stems along in its wake. New clumps catch, and soon the northeast corner is walled in by flames taller than I. My pace quickens, my heart racing. The primordial kid in me has been loosed. The burn is on.

I back up the hill, into thin trees, a rock-strewn landscape, drawing the fire with me.

I look to the south where my husband has begun a fire with his match. I wonder if he used just one. He is more experienced than I, but I am more competitive, more reckless. The fire here is spotty, but the west pasture, only paces away, sprawls for ten or more acres, laden with duff from two years without fire. He is far from me, and if I get into trouble I am on my own.

The fire jumps the fence and threatens a dead tree. I squeeze between barbed wire and catch my jacket, cursing my bulky awkwardness. Flailing, then free, I beat the flames into dead, flat ashes, and by trampling them into submission avoid our neighbor's ire.

The fire has moved into the pasture. It is ahead of me now. I run to keep up with it. On its edge, the heat sears my face, steals oxygen from my lung blood. I gasp as if drowning and lurch backward out of its ravenous grasp. It relents and backs off, like a predator waiting for its prey to weaken. But it never closes in for the kill. It reverts to a domesticated form and does what I intended it to. The burn succeeds, and I am here to tell you about it.

I walk through the embers, loosen smoldering horse manure, rake persistent coals into a hail of sparks that fly up and then extinguish themselves midair. A deer skeleton, long since cleaned of flesh, charred, and disarticulated, is once again visible. I had walked by it often, never seeing it until now. Burnt elytra of beetles and tiny pyramids of soil granules from nesting ants memorialize the cleared landscape. But there are no dead animals, no crisp corpses to testify to the horror of fire. In prairie burns, the birds, deer, and coyote move out, while skunks and badgers lie waiting in burrows deep enough to avoid the inferno above.

I look up. Hawks have come to this part of the sky. They know that not all animals have escaped, or they are waiting for the saved ones to emerge into an exposed hunting ground. Smart birds.

My son and daughter-in-law helped us burn prairie two years ago. She, from Connecticut, had never experienced this rite of spring, but became the best practitioner of all. She refused to leave a section unburned and nurtured each blade with tinder until all had been reduced to carbon. The pleasure of accomplishment shone in her eyes, reflecting the glow of her mission.

This spring, again, we will burn our land. The horses will watch attentively and move easily to safe ground. We'll accelerate the recycling of nutrients and give the new grass room and light and heat from the sun-absorbing black blanket of burnt ground. We will be good stewards of the prairie. We will be reenacting a ritual practiced by early settlers, keeping it and the prairie alive and vital. The world will become strange and wonderful again, like it was when we were kids. And the spring housecleaning will wait.

Night Fires

Carolyn Hall

My headlights trace asphalt seam
through deserted Flint Hills.
Night air hints of sweet embers.
An orange halo crowns the next rise.
Radiant flames bookend my path.
Yellow capped crimson streaks
dance into a moonless sky. Mesmerized
by the celestial flare, I slow to watch
the ebb and flow of serpentine blaze.
Amber glazed clouds of smoke cascade
around me. Purged by fire,
this tallgrass prairie
sustains through generations.
Past and present converge:
Sacred space, holy dimension,
nature's pyre unleashes primal essence.
Buffalo hooves thunder. Shadows
of wild mustangs stampede through the hills.
Night birds take flight above
haunting melodies of cedar flutes.
Earth drum beats nature's rhythm, distant
voices chant stories into the future,
past the mirage of the moment,
beyond the speed limit of sight.

The Barrier

Rafe Montello

*T*he sun dropped to the horizon, pulling me toward it as it fell. I wanted to turn around and head back home, but I couldn't. I said I would be there. I had committed. More embarrassing than not participating would be not to go at all. I settled back, again, determined to get there. Driving the forty miles west of Madison, I make the crisp right at Dodgeville. It was a trip I had made many times before, since I used to camp at the nearby state park. I would need to watch for Woods Hollow Road and then the actual location after the turn.

But finding the place was of little consequence. I was consumed with the thought of everyone watching and judging me, wondering whether I would find the courage to join in.

I turned the heater back on as I entered Dodgeville. I should have eaten before I left. But how could I? Even now I wasn't hungry; I just shivered sporadically.

I read the directions again. The turnoff was exactly 4.2 miles past the center of town. I noted the reading on the odometer. Soon I was out of town. The shadows from the trees on the left were rapidly losing their distinction as they merged with the encroaching darkness. Nightfall only accentuated my uncertainty.

What was I so afraid of? Margaret, the teacher, had assured me I didn't have to take part.

"Don't worry. It will either be your time or it won't. Let the fire tell you what to do. Don't force yourself. I've seen some nasty burns when people force themselves before they're ready."

Would I be ready? I wasn't ready now. What difference could a few hours make? I released the breath I had been holding. How did I let myself get involved in this?

Stupid question. I've been drawn to the new and unusual for as long as I can remember, especially when it came to testing myself. When I saw the flyer at my local food co-op, I knew I had to go and at least watch. I didn't anticipate joining in. I also didn't anticipate Margaret telling me the price was the same either way. By that point, I felt too far in to back out.

"I'll be there."

Why? Why can't I learn to listen and think before opening my mouth?

My inner debate burned so that I almost missed the turnoff. At the start of the gravel road, I began marking the 2.3 miles to the McQuinly farm. Once I arrived, I parked on the grass, away from the other cars. As usual, I arrived late.

Inside the farmhouse, I met the others, paid my fee, and signed the waiver of liability. I scrawled my signature and reflected: nobody would force me to walk barefoot over fifteen feet of blazing coals, nobody but myself and social pressure.

The teacher was a little older than I, but the rest of the group was in their twenties. Most were still in college, except for the dreadlocked Sam and his girlfriend, the self-named Patchouli Flowers.

The two of them had relegated formal education to the dustbin of irrelevance and were trying to eke out an existence selling a hodgepodge of their creative endeavors. They played music, made pottery, and sold fresh herbs to the organic groceries in town. Dressed in a pastiche of ill-fitting clothes, I wondered if they also sold a little ganja to make ends meet. No matter. I was glad to see the cultural revolution I had embraced so many years ago lived on in the hearts and minds of a new generation.

Margaret led us outside to the grassy area where we built a large fire. She reminded us that we didn't have to walk. "Let the fire tell you whether you are ready."

Perhaps some of the others shared my concern, or was she speaking only to me?

"Everyone should choose a log and put it in the fire. That is your connection, your communication to the spirit of the blaze."

I grabbed the largest chunk I could find. I doubted that the fire could communicate to me, but if it did, I wanted to make sure I would hear what it had to say.

Over the next couple of hours, while the fire blazed and then died down, we did a round robin on what we hoped to gain by the experience, held hands, sang songs, chanted, and meditated upon the glow in front of us. I almost forgot my fear, although periodically I turned away from the fire to warm my back.

When the tongues of flame had stopped on all but a few pieces, Margaret raked the coals into a bed over twelve feet long.

"Now is the time," she proclaimed as she kicked off her shoes and walked to the top of the coals. "I'm going to do an Irish jig tonight."

With little hesitation, she jigged her way down the entire length. I blinked several times as she danced, one step so wild it sent a coal careening across the grass. She finished the jig, stepped calmly on the grass, and walked toward us. Her feet seemed fine.

"Who's next?" she invited.

Sam removed his shoes and socks, as did several others. Mine remained on. With no hesitation, Sam strode down the glowing bed. I marveled at his calm. The others followed, not quite as confidently, but they did walk.

I stood transfixed by the glowing heat. The intensity of the red seemed to fade in and out as if the fire were breathing. I stepped closer. What was I afraid of? The others did it. Patchouli stepped up and walked without hesitation across the coals. When she stepped off the end, she turned and smiled at the group as she walked back to Sam.

I removed my shoes and socks and approached the top of the coals. Everyone was watching. I couldn't turn back now. Inhaling, I closed my eyes and stepped into the unknown. Moments passed. My feet were moving. I opened my eyes. I was half way down the bed of coals. I was walking on fire.

I walked twice more that night. My feet were a little swollen and red, but otherwise fine. One of the group received a quarter-size burn. Sam wanted to walk across the coals on his hands, but Margaret talked him out of it.

After the fire died down and we extinguished the remnants, we went back inside the house. Margaret passed out bumper stickers that read "I walk on fire. I can do anything." On the ride home I felt curiously alive and energetic. My feet throbbed. The heater stayed off.

Firewalkers will tell you that the feat demonstrates mind over matter. Scientists offer explanations like the sweat on the bottom of your feet changes to steam, which dissipates the heat without causing injury. But what about the steam, doesn't that burn?

I don't know if firewalking demonstrates mind over matter, but I do know it demonstrates mind over conditioning. From our earliest days, we are raised to believe fire will burn us. But such conditioning interferes with a more direct and authentic experience of reality. And each barrier we remove brings us that much closer to living a life of honesty and fulfillment.

Phoenix Rising

J. Eva Nagel

*C*hange comes in many forms. There are the changes that sneak up on you from behind when you are distracted by an untied shoelace or a pile of dirty dishes. There are changes that can come like a sprite in the night urging you to pack your bags and move to Sedona. Sometimes change saunters in like an unemployed hustler in cowboy boots and has his way with you. Not being a particularly subtle woman, I seem to get the version of change that hits you over the head with a frying pan and squawks, "Yoo-hoo, move your butt over here."

I have heard it said that the world will end in fire. I was presented with this scorching form of change in the middle of the night, in the middle of autumn, in the middle of my fiftieth year. My house burned. Not down exactly . . . more like up.

One quiet Sunday evening I retired to bed completely engrossed in my ordinary, albeit frenzied, life replete with shoulds, musts, and highly significant ought-to's. My appointment book eagerly rested on the table brimming with expectations.

A few hours later, I was bedless, clothesless, homeless, and appointment free.

Have you ever thought of this possibility? Here's how it went for me: OK, if there's a fire, first get the kids out, then the animals. If there is any time left, go for the photo albums. Now this "save the photo albums" plan sounds simple, right? I pictured tucking them under my arms and running out of the house. Well, think again. I had been raising four kids and various additions for twenty-seven years. Even for a sporadic chronicler of photo opportunities, that's a lot of pictures. And sixteen photo albums do not easily fit under two arms. There I was—my house burning—and I was standing in the hall with one album tucked under each arm, fourteen to go. What did I do? I moved toward the guest room away from the fire. Wait a minute. What if the whole house burns down? I know, I'll dump them out the back door. Naaa. The fire hoses might soak them. I stood there swaying with indecision. Finally, I raced to the back door, dumped out the recyclables, loaded in the photo albums, and dragged the bin out into the yard.

I was doing great, but this is as far as my scenario ever got—the children, the pets, the photo albums were safe—now what? I turned toward the shelves of books and it hit me: I am going to lose all of you. My life was in those shelves: the books on childbirth, gardening, environmental issues, an entire shelf on Waldorf education, women's issues and healing guides. Native American religion, a huge collection of fairy and folk tales, another of poetry. What about the biographies? And the novels! The ones I loved and passed to my sons and daughters: *The Lion, the Witch and the Wardrobe; Siddhartha; Grapes of Wrath; The Bean Trees; A Story Like the Wind; House of Spirits.*

I took a deep breath and whispered, "You were terrific, I have loved you, now I bid you goodbye." A feeling of floating free crept into me. All those books had accumulated a great deal of dust. I had so many clothes I couldn't decide what to wear in the morning. I had too many electrical gadgets: toasters, juicers, waffle irons, boom boxes, and answering machines. These things were not me. I could do without them. I pictured myself setting forth into the rest of my life, free and unfettered with nothing to tie me down and fray my soul.

If I were a bona fide flower child, my story would end here, and I would be living in a yurt on the ashes of my house with a few charred pots and a warm sleeping bag, dispensing wisdom in short, easily digestible segments. The truth is a lot messier and much less picturesque. After the fire was put out, my books were still there, though they were wet and smelly. The house did not burn down; it merely burned. It did not turn into purified dry ash and blow away in the wind; it turned into a sodden, reeking mess. The alchemy failed: my lead did not turn into gold; it merely melted. My life was not liberated and simplified but complicated and inconvenienced.

"We will live simply," my rather simple-minded husband said. "We don't need much." Explain to me how I live simply with three jobs, two offices, doctoral thesis deadlines, volunteer responsibilities, three rental units, a hungry teenager, two cats, a dog, and a turtle. Someone had better break it to him gently: those carefree Woodstock days are long gone.

Did I mention my research papers? I was close to the final approach on my doctoral thesis. To this glorious end, I had amassed a three-foot stack of photocopied research articles sorted by categories. Most of these survived the fire (yay!) but not the fire hoses (boo!).

I despaired at the smelly, sodden mess. The next night, over sushi, the man at the next booth told me to put them in the freezer. It will stop the rotting process and buy me some time. Thank goodness for good friends!

I arrived at Jane's house dragging two garbage bags filled with sticky, crumbling papers. They fit perfectly between the pop tarts and the turkey. There they wait until I am settled in a rental house with an oven.

I then began peeling and baking my papers in small slices. Just as with pancakes, the skill is in the flipping: not too soon or the dampness will cause mildew and not too late since the smell of charred paper does not whet the appetite. If you open the office closet and inhale you will find my resurrected research.

Friends ask how our fourteen-year-old son is doing. I do not know. After the first confused weeks sleeping in various places, he seemed completely unaffected. He was involved in his own life and this did not seem to place that high on the Richter scale. Until one day almost two months after the fire, he says, "You know what I really miss?"

I think, oh boy, here it comes at last. He has buried this for so long.

"No, what is it honey?" I ask with tender parental concern.

"Tall glasses." He answers form the depths of his soul.

"Tall glasses?" I gulp in confusion.

"Yup. The glasses we have here are too small for a good drink."

OK, so much for deep inner healing. Soon afterward, I located a couple of tall glasses for his liquid pleasure.

❦

Annie Lamott says that courage is fear that has said its prayers. Maybe the twenty-four years of family songs and prayers, tears and laughter, joys and sorrows under those 250-year-old living-room beams counted for something, because we never felt afraid. This is not a story of tragedy. Tragedy is babies suffering. Tragedy is mothers dying young. Tragedy is planes crashing and buildings crumbling. This fire was not a tragedy. I keep searching for a word that is stronger than inconvenience, but less than disaster. Instead, I am left with the words of a well-fed bear: "Oh bother."

Maybe this will become the story of the phoenix, the one who rises from the ashes, dusts herself off, spreads her wings, and flies off into the sunset. Here I am in the second half of my life, my children mostly grown, expectations becoming clearer, life settling into comfortable routines. And I get this wake-up call in the middle of the night. OK. I am wide awake. I am paying attention. I see friends who rallied support: food, blankets, and all the extra attic furniture. I see a family unified and ready to celebrate. I see a husband who makes each drama into the latest new adventure. I see blessings everywhere I turn. I see how transformation creeps into the roofless house of my being and pushes me out to greet it.

So watch out for me. I am rising from the ashes—dusty and a wee bit discombobulated, but ready to fly. Next time I will ask for ice instead of fire, or at least a brick house, but until then, this fire will definitely suffice.

In Search of Fire

nwenna kai

$\mathcal{A}$strologically my sun sign is Scorpio (water), Taurus rising (earth), and my moon sign is Aries (fire). Even though I believe that astrology is a map, not a destiny, my elemental makeup has put me in search of fire my entire life.

I grew up in a working-class neighborhood in Philadelphia with b-boys and homegirls. Even though I wasn't part of that world, I observed it closely. I was drawn to the homegirls in my neighborhood. They screamed FIRE with their quick slang, their hip styles of dressing, and their flirty mannerisms. I also grew up with a mother whose fiery temper scared me right out of the house and off to college. I have never looked back.

It is ironic, though, that since I left this neighborhood, my home, and this fire, I have been in search of that same fire, wondering how I could take that energy and turn it into something that would move me further into divine purpose.

During my first years in college, I suffered from depression and acute lower back pain that left my sciatic nerve in constant pain. After bouncing through doctors and other forms of treatments, I discovered kundalini yoga.

In my first class, I got in touch with the fire through *breath of fire*, a rapid inhalation and exhalation of the breath through the abdomen. It was the first time in my life that I really felt energy moving in my body. For the first time, I could feel the back of my eyes, the twist of my hips, and the heat in my heart. I discovered, through doing the daily asanas, meditations, and chanting, that fire lives inside of us at the base of the spine. All we have to do is to ignite it.

What is interesting about all of the elements— water, air, earth, and fire—is that they have both productive and destructive qualities. When we think of water, we think of calming, soothing, emotional qualities, but water can be very destructive. Think of what physically happens when water floods your basement. When we think of fire, we immediately think of destructive qualities. When we put fire to our foods, it kills the vitamins and minerals.

We teach our children to beware of fire, to not play with matches and to not play at the stove, but fire moves us. It ignites passion. It drives us to fight for justice and peace. It also puts us in the moment. If there were a fire in your house right now, think about how present in the moment you would become. Fire has the ability to move us to our Truth.

Fire moves me to divine purpose and action. Fire moved me to Los Angeles to pursue my dream of writing and producing for television and film. Fire moved me to heal myself from within. Fire moved me to make significant changes in my life.

Instead of being afraid of fire, I celebrate fire in all ways. I wear bright reds and oranges. I douse my food with cayenne pepper and drink hot tea on those desert hot days in Los Angeles. I retreat to saunas and sweat lodges to detoxify my body.

I fall into trances from doing fire meditations where I gaze at a burning candle while visualizing the flame inside of my heart. After a while, I somehow slip away from my body and disappear into the flame, going to a place where I am the fire burning and moving all at the same time.

Occasionally, when the mood strikes me, I sunbathe in my yard, soaking up all of the fire from the sun. I crave warm bodies, warm kisses and hugs, and the fire that human bodies exchange through touch. I surround myself with fiery guitar rock beats and thunderous drum music, dancing and spinning around my room while feeling fire shoot up my spine. This is the fire that I celebrate. The same fire that moved me away from familiar places and people is the fire that keeps me alive and present.

Fiery Bath

Jennifer Brown

I was feeling a little frazzled. The housework was piling up, the kids fighting, the dinner unmade. I was tired from running my eleven-year-old from sporting event to Scout meeting, and spent from entertaining my artistic three-year-old. And six months of nursing my new baby left me outright exhausted.

I kept up the pace for months, telling myself that being a stay-at-home mother was my choice and that I was enjoying it so much I couldn't get tired. *I'll relax when I'm old*, I told myself day after day, my footsteps slowing and my eyes resting on dark purple circles. Despite my mantra, I was becoming wearier with every errand, job, and chore thrown my way. It was clear that I needed a break.

My husband splurged when we built our house and paid for the two-person Jacuzzi bathtub in the master bedroom, much to my delight. Back in the days of only one child, I used that tub often, curled up in it with a book, dozing to the lull of bubbles. For the better part of two years, however, the only time I stepped foot in that tub was to wash away the dust that had collected. As I cleaned it week after week, it looked like a tempting way to relax, and my worn-out thoughts began to turn to the tub.

My first night in the tub was disaster. The baby woke up just as I eased into the water and I had to trot, dripping and wrapped in a towel, to his crib to soothe another bout of colic.

The next night I tried again, with the same pathetic results. I couldn't relax as I heard things crashing in the kitchen and imagined what calamity would be facing me once I got out of the tub.

I tried turning the hot water heater to a higher temperature, sipping hot tea from fancy china, adding bubble bath, but nothing worked. Something was missing. Something that could help me relax.

Finally, one night as I was readying myself for my nightly bath failure, I had an idea. I rushed to the kitchen pantry and loaded my arms with every candle I could find. Old votives I'd forgotten, Christmas candles, leftover wedding tapers.

"I'm taking a bath," I announced to the family, as I grabbed a box of matches. "Nobody bother me."

I lined up the candles along the sides of the tub while it filled, then turned out the light and slipped in. Slowly, I lit each candle. One for the spilled Cheerios in the dining room. One for the oil stain on the driveway. Two for teething. Another one for the clothes I forgot to pick up at the dry cleaners. And one, the biggest one, to commemorate the last time my husband and I were alone together.

I watched the flames flicker in the darkened bathroom, reflecting in the window and on the water, turning all the tiny bubbles into gleaming fish eyes. I felt them warming me, giving my skin a healthy glow and making me look and feel younger in its light. I turned on the Jacuzzi and watched the flames jump with the vibration of it. They looked like they were dancing and I began to tap my feet under the water.

I tossed my book over the side of the tub to the floor and concentrated on the dancing flames instead. They brought warmth to everything I'd done that day, erasing the sharp edges from the toughest of the day's deeds.

Under the candlelight, the latest clothing crisis of my daughter's turned into a beautiful premonition of her growing to be a woman. The finger paint on the dishwasher melted into a treasured one-of-a-kind piece of art that only my oldest boy could create. The upcoming night of waking to nurse softened into an opportunity to cuddle my baby.

I stayed in the tub until the water cooled and the candles nearly burned themselves out, and only then did I slowly and reluctantly pull myself out, ready to face the work on the other side of the bathroom door. But my communion with the soft firelight of the candles made me newly aware of how much I loved being a stay-at-home mom and gave me renewed strength and vigor in my love for my life. As I toweled off, a smile on my face, I made a mental note to stop by the store the next day. I had to stock up on candles for the next night's fiery bath.

Bush Fire

Jessica Hankinson

My parents met when my dad, the new chemistry teacher, wandered into the school library looking for a match to light his Bunsen burner. My mom, the librarian, didn't have a match, but sparks flew that day in the high school library in Geneva, Ohio.

Twenty-five years later, I was staring at the blue flame of another Bunsen burner. Unfortunately, there was no shortage of matches. I dipped my tweezers in the beaker of alcohol and held them in the flame. It spread down the sides of the tweezers, and I felt the stinging heat through my latex gloves. I let them cool and carefully transplanted another seed into the sterile medium. Ninety-two more to go.

Taking after my Dad, part of me was thrilled to be here, in an Australian agriculture laboratory halfway around the world. Taking after my mom, another part of me longed to return to the Institute's library and curl up with a copy of *New Scientist*.

As I pulled up a new seed, the tiny nugget of life slipped out of my tweezers and fell on the countertop. Contaminated. Worthless.

Can't I do anything right? I bike to work on the wrong side of the streets. I walk up the wrong side of the stairs. I write the dates backwards on my seed packets; how many more times will I forget 3/8/00 means August 3? And what happened to my so-called boyfriend? I'm not worth the twenty cents per minute phone call?

No worries echoed in another part of my brain. I'd heard this phrase for the first time when trying to get telephone service in my subleased apartment. "No worries," he'd said when I'd forgotten the name of the street I was living on. "No worries," he'd said when I apologized for not having paper and a pen ready.

"No worries," I calmed myself later that weekend, when I began to wonder if a young woman taking a walkabout alone was such a good idea. I was on an isolated section of a bike path where a bush fire had ravaged a section of the eucalyptus forest. As I walked further, the blue-green leaves yielded completely to blackened, singed trunks. Then, to the right of my path, I noticed a straggly adolescent tree. While the fire had destroyed the rest of her neighbors, this lone tree had somehow remained unharmed. A single tree had been spared.

How could that tree still stand so triumphant, so proud? Wasn't fire always all-consuming?

I realized that during that long first month, the fire in my soul had only seemed all-consuming. Any effort at joy seemed pointless and I could only count down the days till my return home. But that tree reminded me that no matter how intense the burning in your heart, some part of your soul is spared.

During the walk back into town, I searched for the part of my soul that was scorched, yet still triumphant and alive. Although during that long month I had been focused on my loneliness, frustration, and pain, I had also experienced amazement and wonder.

I remembered the thrill of my first day, seeing parrots on the sidewalk and kangaroos in the backyard. And there was still so much left to explore and experience in this strange new place.

In two weeks, I had tickets for a long weekend in Melbourne, and I'd see the giant fruit bats that presided over the botanical gardens. And tonight, if the skies stayed clear, I'd look up at the sky and see Orion standing on his head.

This Burning

Dane Cervine

In the dark ahead, it floats like an orange mirage,
eerie flame of light in the hills that surround Los Angeles
like taut, brown undulations—
driving back from a conference
about youth, abused & neglected—how the world swims
in alternating waves of fierce light & infinitely dim
shades of despair. The plenary speaker with his grim tale
of childhood—the rapes, the abuse—how the system
saved his life, foster parents lifting him up
far enough to stand on his own DNA & the mysteries
of karmic spirit carrying
his story to the *New York Times*,
his work to three presidential citations for excellence.
And the road winds higher
through the night as the orange glow
grows brighter, flames lapping the black outline of
swelling ground—
still too distant to be afraid—but the awe growing.
As when I met Azim—
Persian born in Africa, educated in England,
financial consultant turned crusader against the violence
that took his son in the streets
of San Diego, college student

delivering pizza unfazed by the bogus address
in the run-down neighborhood,
the 14-year-old gang-banger
waiting for him with the gun, told he'd become a man
by taking the other one down.
And in the aftermath,
Azim finding the 14-year-old boy's grandfather, saying
my son's death must come to mean something—
how they banded together bent
on saving at least one more,
and another, then another. How his eyes burned
as I shook his hand, thanked him for his story,
told him it means everything—how I drove silently
in the night into the heaving hills afire, so close now,
not knowing if there would be a way through,
the black asphalt road leading inexorably
into the smoke-orange flame of the grapevine,
the only way out being through—and there it was,
the fire-break, the very road I was on, separating
Hades' heat on one side from the quiet untouched hills
on the other. In between, in this eerie safety
of windshield & engine & wheels, I see
there is but one way to travel this world,
and it is toward, not away,
from this burning.

Bridges of Light

Jan Phillips

Editor's note: Jan Phillips, photographer and author of several inspirational books, was in a near-fatal car accident while returning from a retreat/photo shoot in Death Valley and Yosemite National Park. She was standing in front of her car, which was off road, to videotape a flock of stunning birds. Another driver hit the back of Jan's car at 70 miles per hour. Jan's car hit her, catapulting her into the air. She landed in a ravine next to the road, the depression of land saving her life. Her car landed over her, muffler and exhaust system burning her right back, right hip, and right elbow severely. She had third-degree burns and extensive skin graft surgery. She wrote the following message to her friends and newsletter recipients.

*D*ear hearts, first I want to thank you for your prayers, your candles, and cards and messages of comfort and joy. I absolutely believe that it is your love and energy that enables me to sit here in this chair and be with you for these few minutes, sending back to you my own fire and prayers of gratitude.

The doctors say the skin graft is doing well. Physically, I am healing well, though it feels sometimes like glass is growing in my back instead of new cells. I'm struggling with panic/anxiety/post-traumatic images so am asking that you still keep me in your prayers and keep the candles burning. I appreciate all your reiki, all the waving of your magic wands, all the ringing of the bells, all the sounds of my name on your lips as it makes its way to the Most High and Deep.

As you might have suspected, I have been mining this for meaning, all the while knowing it is moot, that the meaning is to accept the reality of each moment as another facet of God. Just that and no more. But still I search and scour my memories, knowing there must be a jewel in there somewhere—like a child in search of that colored egg in the bush, that gold coin in the velvet pouch. And I have found something—not the meaning, not the "why" behind this mystery, not the point, but a clue—I have found a clue, and here it is:

When I was under the car, trapped and being burned by the muffler and exhaust system, I was aware that I was facing the moment of my death. I was fully conscious and chose to go calmly, like the Eskimo who lies in the snowdrift and falls asleep when it is time. I felt that I had done a good job with my life. I prayed for everyone I was leaving behind. I thanked God for the richness of my experience, then I closed my eyes and waited for the passage to begin.

Only moments later, I heard the sound of men's voices.

"Is anyone there? Is someone alive?"

"Yes, I'm here, under the car."

"Oh my God! Someone's alive under there! What do we do now?"

I saw their feet moving in one direction, then another. They had no idea what to do.

"Hold on!" one said. "Stay there. We'll go get help."

"No," I said quietly. "YOU are the help. Don't go anywhere. Just lift up the car."

And in one miraculous moment, they became the gods we are capable of being. They put their hands under the fender, and on the count of three, lifted the car as if it were an eagle's feather. I crawled out from under, and have been on the healing path ever since.

The clue is that we ARE the healers, we ARE the help—only we have been taught the opposite for so long, that we need to be constantly reminding each other that this is the case. Divinity is coursing through us every moment—it is the sacrament of our lives. Whatever is needed—love, strength, compassion, wisdom—we have these things within us. We are deep wells of light when we are true and open to our own sacredness. Those men knew it the moment I reminded them. They knew it in their cells and they saved my life by believing in their power and light.

And each of you, as you pray for me and all those you are praying for, or sending energy to, or loving from afar—each of you are doing the healing work—healing wounds of the body and soul, wounds of the heart and mind—and your day will come when we, the recipients, turn our light on you in your hour of darkness and you'll feel it, you'll know the feeling of faith, the touch of Light.

So thank you, my kinfolk, my sisters and brothers in spirit—thank you for getting me this far, and thank you for helping me through the next few months. I need you and I feel you there in so many ways. This is the greatest grace of my life. This communion. This community. These bridges of light from one of us to the other. Blessed be.

All my love, jan

Firewater

Carol Shenold

Suppertime with two active grandchildren is a challenge that can keep me hopping, especially when everyone wants something different. I'm always trying to be the organized one, keeping on task at all cost so we can efficiently finish and move on. I'm not a spur-of-the-moment kind of gal. Even so, in the middle of fixing tacos and quesadillas one October Sunday evening, I pointed out a particularly wonderful sunset to seven-year-old Megan.

"Megan, look. The sun's going to catch the lake on fire."

"It is not. The lake is water."

She looked at me as if Grandma had lost her mind. Her sister, Nikala, intently watched the Disney channel and ignored us.

"I mean it. You want to see?" I turned the fire off under the quesadillas and taco meat.

Megan looked out the kitchen window. "We can't even see the lake from here."

"That's right, but we can go to the lake." Lake Overholser was only a block away from the house. "But we'll have to hurry if we don't want to miss it."

Megan looked at the food on the stove. "Right now, in the middle of cooking?"

"Sure," I said, thinking fast, not always my strong suit. "Everything will keep. Nikala, do you want to come too?"

Nikala shook her head no, engrossed in her show.

"OK. Go tell Grandpa we'll be right back."

Megan and I jumped into the car and drove down to the lake. I parked and we picked our way down to the water's edge so we could see without trees in the way. Grackles and starlings chattered in the trees as they settled in for the night. A few gulls still soared close. One pelican flew home with a beak full of dinner.

The sky turned turquoise. Clouds shaded into coral, then gold, then orange, each color more intense than the one before. The sun settled closer and closer to the edge of the earth. On the other side of the lake, dark tree arms reached up to snare the sun on its way, trying to make the light stay longer. Finally, the sun rested on the edge of the lake and set the sky and lake on fire. Fire crept across the lake until we were bathed in color, our skin rosy and glowing.

I picked up Megan, silent for once in her life, and wrapped her up with me in my fire-colored sweater. We cuddled together and absorbed colors into our souls, soaked in fire that didn't burn, and breathed in cool October air, scented with burning leaves.

Later, when we sat down to a supper that had to wait thirty minutes later than usual, Megan bubbled over with the light and colors and birds. Supper tasted even better than usual and the world didn't end because I didn't meet my schedule.

I won't say that the visit to the lake made me give up my task-oriented ways and become a spontaneous person who always left supper on the stove at the drop of the sun. I won't promise that Megan will become a nature lover from now on. But Megan will notice a sunset now, or point out a cardinal in the backyard.

I wouldn't trade that few minutes bathed in lake fire with Megan for anything. I'd like to think I'll remember to give in to impulse once in a while and catch one of those moments that never come again and hold it in my hand.

Feeding the Fires

Deborah Davis

O ur first night out, we all got cold feet. With the temperature dropping into the forties below zero, not one of our group of four stayed warm.

On our second night, again the air was biting cold, raking my lungs with each breath I took, sneaking icy fingers down my jacket when I shifted my position next to the fire. It was a fire that did nothing. *Nothing.* The heat I felt on my shins didn't counter the cold creeping up my back and down my torso and arms.

My friends felt just as miserable. It was December 31, and we were sitting around a blazing, crackling fire that sent sparks and smoke into the forty-five-below-zero Minnesota night. Each of us sat hunched over, our foursome in a stationary orbit around the leaping yellow-orange flames, trying to get as close to the heat as possible without burning our clothes. But what good was the fire on our faces and knees when it reached only skin-deep? When every part of me except those small patches closest to the flames was shivering?

"You're too quiet," declared Jeannie, our leader and a long-time Minnesota Outward Bound instructor. She made us stand, made us leave the fire, made us tromp down a large circle in the foot-deep snow. The moon was rising; we didn't need flashlights. The lake that held us, the snow covering it, the crystal shards of frozen air piercing our noses, our cheeks, our lungs, all of this was lit cruelly by the white glow of the moon. Jeannie made us run around that circle, hoping we'd create heat in our bodies.

It didn't work. At forty-five below, the heat generated by your churning legs and pumping arms is cancelled out by the additional frigid oxygen you inhale at the demand of those working muscles.

Though the temperatures rose slightly after several days, I barely kept the deep Minnesota cold at bay. I never stood still, wolfing my hunks of cheese and butter-rich logan bread as I moved, skiing vigorously across lake after lake. Once we left camp we took breaks only to warm someone's frost-nipped toes under the shirt and against the bare skin of another's belly. Nighttime was a meticulously orchestrated ritual: disrobe in my sleeping bag, lay my thick wool clothes and boot liners under me to insulate against the cold ground, warm my feet on the plastic bottle I filled with hot water.

Every night I woke after several hours to brilliant stars, icy feet, pressure in my bladder, and a sinking heart. I knew there'd be no more warmth or sleep until I'd peed. In subzero weather, the human body cannot afford to heat a bladder full of liquid.

Like a downhill racer imagining an imminent, treacherous run, I'd visualize first, planning my moves. It was way too cold to hesitate once I was out of the bag. I'd leap out, slip my bare feet into linerless boots, scuttle away from the tarp to pee, dive back into the bag, and hug myself for a long time until I was once again warm and sleepy.

For twenty-one days and twenty nights, I lived from fire to fire. I loathed leaving the breakfast fire until, hauling my heavy pack and working into a rhythm on my skis, I generated a fire within. I dreaded leaving our nightly cooking fires to surrender to my chilly bedding. Like jumping from stone to stone across an icy rushing river, I leaped from one source of warmth to the next, dreading the consequences of splashing between the stones. The fires we built, the finally warmed sleeping bags, the heat rising from inside my down jacket as I swung an axe repeatedly to chop a hole for water in the thick lake ice, all were precious to my seemingly small and vulnerable self in that glacial chill.

One day we skied across a particularly large lake. A strong and bitter wind blew into our faces, snuck through the seams of our jackets, clutched at our vulnerable toes. It wasn't feasible to pause to eat the lunch I always carried in a bag in my pocket. I had to keep moving to fend off the cold. If I was hungry that day, I don't recall it. Keeping in motion was all that crossed my mind.

We chose a campsite on the edge of the lake. Seizing the folding camp saw, I set to cutting dead wood for the evening fire. Dusk fell—it was maybe 4 P.M.—and I sawed with abandon, looking forward to the heat that would build in my body from the effort, heat that would protect me until we had a scorching fire and mugs of hot cocoa.

This evening, however, the exertions of cutting wood did not warm me. I sawed harder, bracing my foot against the log, using my whole body with each stroke. The sky darkened, and my body shivered. I grew colder, and it scared me.

I found Jeannie, who was setting up our tarp. "I'm sawing hard, it usually warms me," I told her, teeth chattering. "But I'm cold and I can't get warm."

"Did you eat your lunch?" she asked immediately.

"C-couldn't," I replied, recalling the fierce wind on the lake. "A bite or two."

Quickly I devoured my leftover blocks of cheese and logan bread. The result was instantaneous and spectacular. Warmth blossomed in my torso, spread upward, downward, out to the far reaches of my numbed fingers and toes. My fear eased. I'd just needed fuel, fuel for my fire. I had no idea the flame had gotten so low.

During those three weeks of bright, crisp days and long, arctic nights, the temperature stayed well below zero—except on one day when it rose to zero and another when it peaked at four degrees. I never missed another lunch on that trip. I dutifully ate a third of a stick of butter in my hot cereal each morning. I came to love my nighttime ritual: one felt boot liner under my knees, one under my hips, my big pink Lopi sweater spread under my torso. I never liked climbing into that cool, unwelcome sleeping bag each night, but I did grow to love the way my own heat could eventually turn it into a comfortable and comforting nest.

I marveled at how potent my own heat was, and yet how vulnerable; how thin the line between my ability to generate heat and my susceptibility to penetrating cold. I learned something about the many appetites of fire and the different fuels that feed them. And I came to appreciate all the fires that we build, the inside ones especially, as well as those that warm us from without.

Fireplace Fantasies

Tammy Murray

"We need to get away," I said.

It was February and it felt like this New England winter would go on forever. The walls were closing in on me. All I did was go to work, drive home in the dark, tend to dinner, do dishes, and I was ready to call it another miserable day. Life was dreary. My husband and I weren't connecting. We talked about bills, schedules, the kids, but it wasn't enough.

"Great!" Tim said. "Let's take some time off and do it!"

Uplifted by his enthusiasm, I began planning. I visualized the scene—a cozy cabin in New Hampshire. We'd be nestled into a big bed with about a hundred pillows covered in beautiful fabrics and laces. We'd spend hours sipping wine, gazing deeply into each other's eyes, and talking. Really talking. We'd talk about our hopes and dreams. We'd plan our future together.

Soon the kids would be off, living their own lives. It would just be the two of us. Did we share a vision of what our life would be like? We should find out. This could be a challenge, though, since we apparently didn't even share a vision of what this long weekend would be like!

For more evenings than I care to remember, I stood over the sink, washing the same dishes I'd washed the night before, listening to Tim bellow from his post in front of the computer.

"Look at this! Four days and three nights in Paris!"

"Tim, we'll come back exhausted. You're not listening to me."

"Yes, I am! You want to get away. Look how cheap this whirlwind tour of Italy is! Can you believe the deals you can find on the Internet?"

I returned to the dishes and my fantasies of snuggling and sharing.

"Tim, you just don't get it."

Luckily for me, Tim is a hopeless romantic. In time, he heard me. He got it. Finally, he turned away from the multitude of bargains and last-minute deals.

"How about this inn in New Hampshire? There are fireplaces in every room." Perfect.

By the time we put our plans into action, February had faded away and March was in full swing. March is a nasty month in the Northeast. With overcast skies above us and mud under our feet, we arrived at my fantasy destination.

"Oh my God, Tim, it's a double bed! It looked so big in the pictures!"

Used to our king-sized bed at home, we wondered how we'd survive three nights in this piece of dollhouse furniture.

The mud quickly dashed our hopes of trying the advertised "cross-country ski trails" that supposedly "begin right at the door of the inn!"

Almost in unison, we heaved a dejected sigh. "Well, at least there's wood. Let's light a fire."

Building a fire together was great practice in diplomacy and compromise. Tim's style of laying the wood in flat, tightly knit layers was clearly the work of a novice. I, a veteran of many summers of camping with my kids, knew better.

"The fire won't get any oxygen if you stack the wood so close."

He built, I adjusted his work, and soon the flames were flickering, then blazing before our eyes. We sat together on the tattered couch, in the tiny, rustic room. As we sat, now somehow fully in unison, we sighed a sigh that was different than the ones from before. This sigh echoed with contentment. In this sigh, my dream weekend came true. The fire had made it happen.

With nothing much to do on a dreary New Hampshire weekend, fires filled most of our time. A lovely meal in the inn's dining room, and then we'd return to the fire. Chilly walks down a country road to drink in the beauty of surrounding mountains, and quickly back to our fire. The hours spent collecting wood, building fires, and finally sitting and enjoying the quiet togetherness, were some of the most special times we'd shared in months.

As we snuggled and watched the flames, we found ourselves opening up. We talked about things we had never discussed before. We shared secret thoughts and feelings. We each let the other into the depths of who we really are. Our spirits, formerly harried and critical of one another, changed. The fire healed the open wounds of recent arguments and neglect. It got under our skin and deeper. It warmed our hearts toward one another. It made us look deeply at each other, and remember how important our relationship is.

❦

It was hard to leave on that final afternoon. We stretched out the last fire as long as we could. Soon the craziness of work, family, and life in general would crowd out the feelings we had found in front of our fires. *If only we could put some of that magical element into a little container, to be opened as needed*, I thought. Imagine if during a hectic day at work we could pull it out of a desk drawer and, just for a moment, feel that deep sigh escape our lips. Or if in the middle of an argument we could sit side by side and stare into the flames. My fantasy had changed from the vision of a cozy weekend to a larger dream. Now I wanted to carry this feeling with me through all my weekends, and weekdays too.

It wasn't long after that weekend that Tim and I decided it was time to sell our house and move out of the city. As we now plan ahead to this change, many concerns and issues arise. How far am I willing to drive to get to work each day? How many cars belonging to kids and their friends can we park in the new driveway? Tim, being a chef, has certain kitchen needs that cannot be ignored. I must have a quiet place to write. The list of our requirements is long. Some things we're willing to be flexible about, and some are written in stone.

What we're sure of, deep in our souls, is that wherever we choose to live, there must be a place where we can retreat together, away from the world, and build a fire. If a fireplace is already there, wonderful! If necessary, we'll build one. We know that the closeness we shared on our winter weekend getaway is something we want in our lives on a daily basis.

We look to the future with excitement. Our hearts and souls were melded together by our cozy New Hampshire fires. We plan to keep them that way. With the help of evenings in front of our new fires, wherever they may be, I know our dreams will come true.

Hearth Fire

Barbara C. Frohoff

In the beginning, burning embers coax us
first with light, then warmth.
By accident, the meat falls off the stick
into the Fire. With gutteral shrieks
it's raked away and torn.
The juices run down toughened faces.

Next, find a hearth inside, under a sod roof.
The Fire beckons, warms cold faces and boots
that draw near as it bakes bread, heats pots
of savory stew on iron hooks.
Pungent woodsmoke fills the spaces,
making brothers, one and all.

Later, elegant marble frames the hearth.
The Fire winks behind the iron grate,
laid by others for the master's pleasure.
In the kitchen the Fire behaves,
knowing its duty, not overreaching,
listening always to tales and tears.

Oh, look! Behind sleek glass doors
the Fire preens and burns,
all dirt and soot shut carefully away.
Proudly civilized, it beckons still,
listens to business deals, late night
proposals, turns wrongs into ashes.

At last, black enamel cups charcoal
as it smolders, lights and glows.
Smoke from fragrant wood chips swirls,
fingering our buried need to gather '-round,
to be enveloped in the hazy smoke, to be
brothers once again, and then
to watch the meat fall back into the Fire.

A Small Orange Flame

Grace Flora

*I*t was a women's empowerment workshop, something many of my friends would shy away from. *Those* friends would not be interested in something so "new age, touchy-feely." But I had *other* friends who were anxious to attend the workshop. We drove out to the countryside, to the retreat location, and met a few other women like us. Ranging in age from our thirties to our fifties, we drank herbal tea out of stoneware mugs and shared our stories. We were not afraid to be empowered— in fact, we would take all the empowerment we could get. Not that we were shrinking violets; our conversations disclosed that we were all accomplished women with good educations and careers.

The workshop leaders guided our group through a morning of meaningful activities and discussions, few of which I remember now. Those activities have paled in my mind not because they were unimportant, but because what came next had such a lasting influence on my life that when I think of that day, I always think about the "burning bowl."

We gathered outside on a small lawn surrounded by trees. The workshop leaders built a small fire in a round barbeque grill. They asked us to think of something we wanted to give up, perhaps something that had been appropriate in the past, but that was no longer helpful for us. We would write this thing on a piece of paper and burn it.

Yeah, sure, I thought doubtfully, *this is really going to work*. But in the spirit of the day, I spent a few moments in contemplation. What came to mind was something I had never before considered giving up.

I had always been proud of the way I handled money. I was so small when I got my first savings account that I couldn't even go on the amusement park rides that said, "You must be this tall." I got my first real job at age sixteen, as soon as I was legal, and I saved most of my pay. (Of course, I had been babysitting for years before that.) My prom dress was not the one of my dreams—it was the one on sale.

I think you get the picture. Between scholarships, financial aid, and my on-campus job I made it through four years of college completely on my own. My parents didn't have to pay for anything, and I wasn't about to ask them to. I bought my first car (used, of course) with cash, and I never went into debt. I was totally self-sufficient; what could be wrong with that? But in those moments of contemplation I sensed that something *was* wrong with that. Perhaps my attitude toward money was limiting me in some ways. On my piece of paper I wrote what I wanted to give up: NOT ASKING FOR MONEY.

In my mind's eye, I can still see the fire scorching the edges of the paper. I had never guessed at the weight of my money pride, but as it was burning away I felt an unexpected lightness come over me.

Now that I'm not afraid to ask for money, I am more empowered and I have helped empower others. There are so many examples, but I'll share just one here. A few years ago one of my students expressed an interest in having the forest activist Julia Butterfly Hill come to our campus. *Too expensive*, my old self would have said, but the new self said, *Why not?*

I encouraged the student to contact Hill's agent and get a date and a price. The price was far too high for any single campus organization to consider, but I visited group after group, administrator after administrator, and *asked for money* to fund her visit. I was not in the least ashamed to ask, and most were very willing to give.

Burning that piece of paper changed my life in many ways. I'm now a more effective fund-raising board member for the nonprofit organizations I work with. I'm not afraid to ask for money for myself either: a refund, a raise. It's only money. I am more generous in giving it to others, too. I burned away my hang-ups about the stuff.

We raised the money for Julia Butterfly Hill to come to our campus. Her inspiring presentation was worth every penny. And when the audience of hundreds rose to give her a standing ovation, my student's face was beaming. We were all empowered that day, and we have a small orange flame to thank.

Meditation: Letting Go with Fire

Maril Crabtree

A large part of living consists of change. Change invariably insists on letting go of something to embrace something else. Yet, most of the time, most of us resist change and resist letting go. We cling to the familiar, no matter how lifeless or unpleasant it may have become. Like the overburdened ant that toils along the path carrying three times his weight in grains of food, we carry it all with us, sometimes toppling with the enormity of it.

I remember a scene from the movie *The Mission* in which Robert De Niro's character, having killed his brother in a fit of jealousy, chains a heavy bag of armor and weapons to his back and carries it with him as penance for his deed. Month after month, he drags the heavy metal behind him. Finally, after De Niro struggles up a mountainside and lies exhausted at the top, others help him cut his burden loose. With grateful tears he watches it tumble down the mountain, knowing he is freed from his guilt.

Sometimes a ceremony or ritual can help us let go, purge, cleanse, and release what needs to be released. One of the most universal ways to let go is with the help of fire.

Fire's way of releasing is to devour, reduce, and transmute. When old feelings, thoughts, beliefs, and emotions hang on beyond their usefulness, it helps to transform their energy by literally watching them go up in smoke.

Native Americans used this method hundreds of years ago. Many ceremonies began with throwing a pinch of tobacco into the smoke of a fire, saying prayers, and watching those prayers mingle with the smoke as they disappeared into the heavens. Native Americans practice the ritual of smudging, lighting a bundle of sweet grass, cedar, or sage, and using the smoke to clear away negative energies and purify the ceremonial space.

Some tribes have ceremonies involving a paho stick, a wooden stick that the participant carves, decorates with feathers or other natural items, and throws into the fire with prayers for release. Many other cultures have ritual burnings of symbolic items to give closure or mark a special event.

In our culture, one popular ceremony is known as the Burning Bowl. Often used to mark the New Year, it is a way to let go of the old year's unresolved issues, failures, and mistakes, to let go of all the ways these negative energies have taken their toll on our minds, bodies, and spirits.

Here is a guided meditation and ritual to create your own letting-go burning-bowl ceremony with the help of the sacred energies of fire:

❦

In a quiet place, with pen and paper at hand, close your eyes and relax. Picture yourself in a dense forest with tall trees, vines, and lots of undergrowth. The trees are so close together that sunlight barely penetrates to the forest floor where you stand. You know you will eventually come to a clearing, and that is your goal: to reach the clearing.

Go forward through the forest. You may be walking, running, or gliding along, but with each movement forward sense the anticipation of coming to that clearing and feel the liberation of making your way through the thick underbrush, leaving behind the gloom.

As you move forward, allow your intuition to show you what needs to be left behind at this moment in your own life. If it's a specific thing or person, bring that into your meditation; if it's something more abstract—fear, for instance, or lack of focus—give it a concrete shape, color, size, and sound. Keep going even if it attempts to block your progress through the forest. Notice how many ways it makes its attempt: it may laugh at you, it may entice you to stop and rest, or try to talk you into finding an easier path. Notice your reactions as you continue to make your way through the forest.

Now you burst into the clearing and see the sunlight streaming onto a fresh, open landscape. Feel the sensation of freedom from whatever burdened you in the forest. Open your eyes and write what you left behind in the forest, what you intend to let go of from this moment on in your life. Contrast your feelings of when this image was present to your feelings when you experienced its absence. Write everything you can remember about going through the forest and into the clearing. End with the words: "If it is in my highest and best interest, I choose to leave behind _____ and I have the power to take whatever action is necessary to accomplish this task."

On a fresh sheet of paper, write the words or draw the image of what you intend to release from your life.

Place the paper in a fireproof bowl and place the bowl on your altar or in another sacred space you've chosen for this purpose.

With intention and deliberation, set fire to the sheet of paper. Use a candle for this purpose (see the Meditation on using candles with intention) or simply use matches. The key is to keep focusing on your intention to release what is on the paper as you watch it burn into ash and smoke. Complete the ritual with an expression of thanks to the universe for providing this powerful tool of fire to help you release and let go.

Part II
Fire Memories

Stories of Recollection and Reminiscence

A Fiery Fall

Maril Crabtree

The fire of fall was at its height that year. The brilliant leaves careened through the air, not caring how or where they landed. They spun in circles on their way down, tumbling on top of each other, like kids playing, building pyramids that collapsed into a tangled mass of bodies.

Leaves rained down on me as I walked, and I thought of how the green of summer is actually the mask. The true colors—the flaming reds, yellows, oranges, and russets—are always there, all year long. They emerge only in the fall as the green fades away. To find its true beauty each leaf goes through an aging and dying process, until finally it lets go and drops through the air, drifting across a vast unknown space.

I thought of how, in their death, these bright fall leaves had at last revealed their sacred inner fire. They sprawled across the sidewalks, looking gay and carefree, and I scuffed through them, listening to their beautiful swish-swish sounds.

Like the fiery colors of fall, we have our true colors. I realized that the process of aging involves the joyous task of exploring one's own true colors, of discovering what they are beneath the summer mask.

Later that year, I celebrated a challenging birthday that plunged me into a whole new decade. It came just one day before solstice. After I celebrated the darkness, I lit all the candles and faced south, the medicine wheel direction of fire and warmth, the place of summer, of the full passions of youth and physical strength. It is also the place of preparation for fall and winter.

I remembered the bright sparks of flying fall leaves as I reflected on how far I had traveled on this medicine wheel. With this birthday, I would once again go into the center of the wheel, the place known as the Children's Fire. Here I would be invited to play with my own curiosity, my own joy and sense of discovery. I could continue to explore my true colors from the safety of this place of childlike wonder, while losing none of the fire of wisdom that comes with age.

I thought of the cleansing fire and steam of the first sweat lodge I ever experienced. I remembered how, each time we greeted the hot stones as they tumbled into the fire pit, they greeted us in return with sparks that flew into the air, and my mind returned to seeing the fall air full of bright sparks of leaf spirits.

After that first sweat lodge, I wrote a poem. The last few lines speak to me still:

Now come the guardian spirits.

They hover from otherworld places,

from South and from East, fire and earth

glowing red in the ebony blanket

that shrouds me. Inside the shell

of the turtle, turning in seven directions,

I spin down the flesh until it is spirit

connected with ancestors' spirit, become

once again a leaf on the sacred tree, ready to fall.

Into the Summer Sun

Peggy Eastman

Overhead, the sun is a fiery orange lollipop with no stick to hold it up, and so it sinks slowly down the sky of its own weight on these long, slow summer evenings. These are the days of almost never-ending bicycle rides on still-steaming asphalt streets with butterscotch glow on bare legs and arms and downhill coasts that create their own breeze to lift our hair off our wet necks. We are riding into the summer sun.

The bicycles talk: tick, tick, tick, ticking faster and faster, and we are pedaling harder as we pick up speed; now there's no need to pedal and we lift our feet. If we go fast enough, we can ride right into the sky and reach out and touch that great orange lollipop—one hand still on the handlebars to keep us steady.

We pause after a downhill coast, cotton shirts moist against our backs, hair clinging to our wet necks, breathing hard from the pedaling, kickstands now keeping our bicycles upright and ready for the ride home, to watch the orange lollipop sink into the gray shingles of a rooftop. The gray-shingled roof eats the lollipop in segments until a quarter of it is gone, then half; the remaining orange sliver lingers on the roof briefly like a jaunty cap until it, too, is swallowed by the gray shingles. When the lollipop sinks, we know we have to head home before the butterscotch glow—soon deepening to burnt copper—turns into a dusky purple.

Today, we almost rode into the sun. If we had pedaled just a little faster, gone just a little farther . . .

But now we must head home to the waiting summer night. These are the evenings of screened windows with one glassed half pulled up as far as it will go to catch a breeze, any breeze at all. These are the nights of stars thrown against the sky like handfuls of popcorn, of instrumental insects and air that wraps itself around us as closely as a lover, as if it cannot bear to let us go. These are the nights of no blankets and sheets kicked off and hair damp against the pillow, moist now not from bicycle riding but from a shower, and an antic insect chorus and the sound of an owl hoo-hooting somewhere high on a tree branch in the backyard. These are the nights of small birds that begin to sing early in the dawn, launching their high notes from somewhere deep in their throats before the sun starts to announce its return with a soft gray morning shawl edged in pink.

We know that someday the almost never-ending days and nights of summer will give way to a pale sun and early winter nights that drop down suddenly with the force of pulled window shades. And what is behind the window shades of those early winter nights we will never know, for that is the season of retreat, of closed houses with storm windows over the glass and screens, and empty spaces on front porches where the cane-seated rockers and wooden swings used to be. In that season, the rockers and swings will have been taken inside, the puffy flowered chintz sitting-pillows put away in the attic or basement in plastic yard bags finished off with twist ties.

And if, in that season of retreat, there are other people behind the storm-windowed houses who also mourn the loss of the large lollipop sun and the long butterscotch-glow bicycle rides, it's not for us to say.

But for now, let's not think about that season of retreat; let's put it far away from our minds, like a postcard of firs in drifted snow pasted in an album placed somewhere far out of reach.

Tomorrow is another almost never-ending day with the return of that fire-filled orange lollipop in the sky, and hills for us to swoosh down, cotton shirts damp against our backs, feet pedaling until the pedals go around so fast, tick, tick, tick, tick, that we lift our feet up and let the gathering speed take us down one hill and halfway up the next.

Tomorrow, we will ride with pumping legs right into the sun, and maybe the season of retreat will never come. We will pedal faster, and we will go farther.

The Kitchen Stove

Claire MacDonell

I grew up in a drafty old house. It was situated on top of a high hill, surrounded by hayfields and forests that extended across the valley and led down to the creek and swamp. When it was built about 150 years ago, it was possible to look straight down to the bay and watch the sea from a window on the stairs. The forest has grown up since then, the view has changed, and the house also fell into ill repair.

When my parents bought the house thirty years ago, it didn't have electricity or indoor plumbing. I remember dragging water from the creek, while my mother remembers that I thought it was just like *Little House on the Prairie*.

My parents believed in raising us in a simple and self-sufficient manner, and that included the design of the central heating system. Our house and hot water were heated by two woodstoves, one in the kitchen and the other in the basement. These large iron stoves were stodgy four-legged beasts, with a draft that creaked open in all weathers and silver-plated spiral handles that became too hot to touch within minutes. There were intricate designs on the door of each stove, embossed with the name of the manufacturer. Each stove rested on its own brick landing, like a throne residing slightly above the common ground.

Besides heating the first floor, the kitchen stove provided a place for my dad's simmering pot of tea and the boiling meat stew he always had on the go. The basement stove was responsible for the hard work of heating the hot water and the rest of the house.

In some form or another, we worked all year to ensure that we had heat for the five months of Canadian winter. My dad spent the summer splitting wood into stove-size chunks, and the whole family would pile it in the basement. I remember sweating in the July sun, disbelieving that winter would ever approach. Yet I felt this momentous responsibility, because if we didn't take in the wood, who would? And if no one took in the wood, we would have no fire, and I would freeze to death, all before my eleventh birthday.

I was impressed that my father needed us, that he would rest such an important task on his children's shoulders. Wheelbarrow by wheelbarrow, we lined the basement with neat rows of wood, getting splinters, jammed fingers, and bruised shins along the way.

My brother's biggest chore was to make little bundles of kindling, newspaper, and cardboard, joined together with masking tape. They were not too tightly wrapped, so that air could circulate and we could get the fire going with one match. Dad put the bundle in the stove, opened the draft, and sent the air whistling down the chimney. He piled chunks of dry hardwood close to the stove walls so that they rested precariously on top of my brother's bundle. Then he'd shut the door and tell us to leave it be, but it took me years to develop the patience to let a fire catch in its own sweet time.

My room was the kitchen loft. Each morning I woke under thick covers of wool blankets and quilts, listening for my father moving in the kitchen. Once I trusted that my father had relit the night's ashes, I dressed underneath the covers and quickly headed to the kitchen.

I silently huddled next to the stove, nudging the cat from her coveted position beside the chimney. I stood so close that the heat cut through my jeans and turned my skin red, while my mother worried that I would light my clothes afire.

This was my favorite time of the day. The oldest of four children, our house wasn't very quiet and I rarely had my parents' attention to myself. On those cold winter mornings I was the first one up, as my dad sat in the rocking chair drinking tea and my mother prepared breakfast. Once I pulled myself away from the seductive heat of the kitchen stove, we ate together and quietly read the newspaper, exchanging sections for the next half hour.

Once the kitchen was toasty warm, I relaxed my shoulders from their shivering tension as my younger siblings piled out of bed and raged downstairs. The sun was poking over the trees when I left the house to catch the school bus.

After an upbringing of taking in wood, huddling close to fire, and feeling warm and safe when everyone was sitting around the stove on a stormy winter's night, I took a job at a wilderness camp for struggling teenage boys in the heart of the Appalachian mountain range. Most of these children didn't go outside for more than ten minutes a day, had felt concrete beneath their feet their whole lives, breathed recycled air full of carbon by-products, and put their prepackaged meals in the microwave. When they arrived at camp, they looked at the simple steel grate and brick firepit built underneath a slanted roof with a wooden bench placed next to it.

"Where's the microwave?" one asked

"There's no microwave," I responded.

"Well, where's the stove? How are we supposed to cook?"

"That's your stove right there," I said, and nodded at the grate with a slanted roof.

He looked at me with a mixture of horror, disbelief, and cynicism.

"That ain't right, man," he muttered as he walked away. I chuckled.

One of the first skills these boys learned was how to build a base to start a fire, meaning how to pile sticks, kindling, and paper together to make the precious timber light into something useful and long lasting. It wasn't much different than my brother's chore.

On his first attempt, I would watch the boy blow and adjust the sticks, holler for more wood, more paper, more cardboard, more ANYTHING to get the fire going. He would usually offer prayers and curses to God and devil, invoking any spirit that might provide light and heat in his crumbling tower of half-charred twigs and paper ashes. So many boys struggled to have patience with the fire, just as I did at their age.

After a couple of failed attempts he would be open to the direction I had to offer, and we would rebuild slowly, carefully placing kindling, small sticks, and cardboard in a square frame, leaving space for the fire to breathe but not enough that it would get hungry and die. We needed that fire to cook that food, and once the bellies started rumbling, mine included, the concentration increased tenfold.

Once the flame caught and the fire roared to life, we breathed with relief and smiled with pride. In these moments, I was able to step out of the role of counselor and authority figure. We were two people with sooty hands, ashes in our hair, and smoke in our reddened eyes, who had worked together on equal ground.

As time went on, the boys learned more efficient systems for warming their food and their bodies, but it always remained a central task of the day to collect enough dry wood of the right size, and to have someone with skill and patience in charge of the cooking fires.

We used the fire at night, but for different reasons. After the day's activities were done, we lit the fire and sat around in a circle to discuss issues or particular problems. Sometimes it can be easier to stare into a fire and let thoughts flow off the flames than to look another person dead in the eye and speak difficult words. As the flames died down, so did the emotions of the evening, and soon the boys settled into bed.

Around smoking embers, I decompressed after a fifteen-hour day, talking, laughing, or crying. Then I threw some water on the fire and left the steaming ashes for a well-earned rest.

From my drafty house in Canadian winters to a small burnt circle in the Appalachians, fire has cut a theme of responsibility, nurture, and patience. It has been a humbling force that I cannot take for granted, but in which I can take comfort and protection. Sometimes we all could use a kitchen stove in our homes.

Dancing with the Fire

Michael Sky

*I*t began raining early in the morning of Memorial Day that year, and the rain kept up through most of the day. My wife Penny and I were living with two friends in a suburban neighborhood in Concord, just west of Boston.

We planned to have the firewalk on our front lawn. We called the local fire department and told them we were having a holiday cookout with a Hawaiian luau-style wood fire. I began to see the rain as a plus, as it would keep our neighbors indoors. I went to the supermarket and bought a case of charcoal lighter, should I need it to keep the fire going.

For the rest of the day we all just sat around the house, shut in by the rain, and quietly freaked out. Someone would stare into a book for ten minutes without registering a word. Or someone would put water on to boil and then stand empty-headed before the tea cabinet trying to remember why. We paced a lot, moving from one room to another with no discernible purpose. And we managed some courageous gallows humor, which sometimes worked a giggling release and other times only served to deepen the gloom.

Our good friend Jonathon just happened to show up that afternoon, in town for the holiday. Jonathon is an engineer and the most logical, rational, linear, left-brain I have ever known. When I told him our plans for the evening, he at first became excited, for he only heard the part about my demonstrating the walk. As I slowly made it clear to him that everyone might walk on fire, his eyes bugged out and he started looking for the exit. I asked if he would like to serve as fire tender, staying outside and keeping the fire going for us while we were inside preparing to walk. He gladly said yes, happy that he could take part and witness the walk without feeling compelled to do something so utterly inconceivable.

Evening finally arrived, as did my friends. Once again, I found myself sitting in a roomful of people waiting to have root canals without anesthesia. However, this time there was no one present (myself included) who really knew that it would all work out.

Fear feeds on fear. If you look to your old friend for reassurance and instead see fear in his eyes, you will tend to feel frightened, which he will spot in your eyes, further frightening him, which further frightens you, which further frightens him . . . and so it went.

By this time, I had come to understand two basic facts about people that almost always hold true at the start of a firewalk. First, we feel disinclined to intentionally move in the direction of pain, unless we have clear social approval, as, for instance, in the case of athletes or dancers. While we might understand and even applaud the marathon runner's contorted features and occasional shin splints, we consider it quite stupid to intentionally *step on a fire and then suffer injury*.

Second, we have a deep, cellular, instinctive relationship to fire and its burning nature: virtually every life form on this planet knows better than to move in the direction of fire, so again, anyone foolish enough to even consider such a practice surely deserves any resulting pain.

Yet my friends and I had our reasons, strong enough to carry us forward in the presence of our doubts and fears, for there we were. Despite a rather clumsy and halting presentation on my part, the evening progressed and our moment with the fire approached. I told them to take a little break while I went outside to see how the fire had managed in the rain.

I found Jonathon keeping his lonely vigil, umbrella overhead, and I took a rake and poked clinically through the fire, attempting to determine whether we had enough coals to do the walk. I felt suddenly blasted with the heat (the fire had done quite well in the rain), with the fire's glowing burst of energy, and my stomach seized up with the outlandishness and undeniable danger of our enterprise. I took a deep breath, put on a happy face, and went slowly back inside, attempting to emanate all-knowing reassurance. My friends later said that I was white with terror.

And so, we proceeded out to the fire.

The rain had lightened to a soft and cooling presence, and a wonderful blessing and balance for our undertaking. We formed a circle, holding hands, except for Jonathon, who stood dry and sensible beneath his umbrella.

The singing began. I took the rake and began spreading the coals: *all this earth is sacred, every step we take, all this life is sacred, every step we take*. As the fiery carpet first spread out before them, I heard a tangible group gasp. Nothing I had said could have prepared them for the intensity of the heat, for the explosion of sparks and smoke, for the solid red-orange sheet of pulsing embers.

Minds boggled, bodies trembled, and our singing grew louder, viscerally driven.

I stood before the coals, my entire life summed up in the profound thought: "Either it works, or it doesn't, here goes . . ." I walked across, no problem! I was then stunned to see one friend following immediately after, and then another, and another.

Whereas the walks during my training had all progressed slowly, half of our group had walked in the first thirty seconds. Whether they had an extreme desire to walk on fire, or an extreme desire to be finished with walking on fire, they were all smiling, and in the space of a minute we had shifted from unthinking terror to exhilarating joy.

I looked over to Penny, who had not yet walked and who was visibly shaking. I had had a dream just before returning home in which my wife, Penny, had stepped forward and burst into flames. I was hoping that wouldn't happen. For her part, she had always steadfastly maintained that firewalking was not her sort of thing at all, and that if her husband hadn't had the temerity to land one in her own front yard she might have forever remained among the blissfully uninitiated. But there it was, and walk she did, smiling brightly all the way into my waiting arms.

We had by then reached the magical shift that most firewalks achieve: the fire had become friendly and inviting, the singing inspired, and the group intensely bonded, with a strong sense that anything was possible.

As if to affirm it all, Jonathon stepped up to the fire, umbrella still raised over his head, and strolled across the coals with wonderful aplomb, the perfect ending to an unforgettable dance. We had just completed an adventure that, years later, continues to provide a wealth of such moments.

Fire Dreams

Kristine Babe

At sunset, my husband, Dan, rolls our portable fire pit to the side of the yard closest to the road and lights a fire. The neighbors begin to arrive as the smoke clears and flames flicker within the metal mesh surround. The adults carry lawn chairs or portable coolers stocked with beer, wine coolers, sometimes even a shaker of martinis ready to pour. One neighbor brings a large thermos of daiquiris to most bonfires, filling plastic glasses for anyone who cares to partake. Some pull coaster wagons lined with a blanket or two for carting home their tired kids later in the evening.

The kids bring flashlights, ready for a game of White Wolf, a spooky, complex form of flashlight tag; they put the marshmallows and other snacks on a camp table near the fire, then hurry off to begin their games. Our kids, Maggie and Sean, greet the new arrivals, and teams begin to form, teams that metamorphose as more kids arrive or disputes break out over the rules of the game or some of them take a break to roast marshmallows or catch June bugs.

The fire crackles and dances; yellow and orange flames overlap and blend above glowing red coals as I take a seat with one of Beth's daiquiris. The conversation grows lively as we bemoan how little we see each other in winter and talk about the Milwaukee Brewers' latest losing streak, Frank and Sally's ugly divorce, Jeff's upcoming fishing trip, Sheila's most recent karaoke debacle, the elaborate carpools running between summer school, swimming lessons and softball leagues, and the travails of digging up half our lawn to repair the septic system. Someone turns on a boom box, and a few people get up to dance, though most just tell stories of adventures we had when the song—Van Halen's "Jump"—was popular.

I pause to look around at my friends and neighbors and realize that though I enjoy their company and our ritual—I hesitate to call it that, yet it seems like one—of gathering around the fire together, what most satisfies me in the end is the fire itself. It never fails: as conversation continues around me, the fire quiets first my tongue, then my thoughts. In stillness, I watch the flames themselves, leaping and falling in their eternal dance. And soon, the fire takes me away, transporting me as did the campfires of my girlhood.

I am nine years old, camping with my parents and brother in Wisconsin's Northwoods near Tomahawk. I watch my father build our campfire in a pit surrounded by a circle of stones. He stacks logs as I gather sticks for kindling from the edges of our campsite. When the logs, balanced like a tepee, stand ready, Dad takes the twigs I gathered and fits them under and between the logs. He strikes the blue tip of a wooden kitchen match against the raspy side of the box.

As if by magic, the flame swells and flares, leaping with such apparent strength that I'm surprised that it extinguishes when it touches the kindling too quickly. Dad strikes another match or two; the twigs are quickly consumed as the logs catch fire. I watch the smoke clear, mesmerized by the leaping yellows and oranges and the wavering heat above the flames distorting my view of the trees at the perimeter of our campsite.

With a marshmallow on a long toasting fork, I hesitate, wary of the fire's hunger. Flames want to lick my marshmallow, to make it, like the logs, dance with flame. I look for the red coals, glowing and already satisfied, not interested in burning my treat. I slowly turn my fork until my marshmallow has a puffy, golden-brown shell. I know it's warm and gooey inside, so I slide it off the fork and eat it in one bite. That way, I don't get my fingers or face sticky. Marshmallow on my fingers or face inevitably ends up in my hair, a sticky knot that brings with it threats of a haircut. My hair hangs in one long, tight braid down my back to keep it out of the fire and away from hazards such as marshmallows.

After a time, the fire lulls me, and I sit back to watch it. I stare into the flames, absorbed in their ever-changing colors and shapes. I watch a log glow red and later darken as ash builds on its surface and the burning moves toward its core. As I stare, I grow still, utterly absorbed in the fire's dance, the heat warming my face until it feels as red as one of the glowing logs.

For a while, my mind is completely filled with the sight, sound, smell, even taste, of the fire. Then the fire leads me beyond itself into dreams and stories and memories, all mixed together, beautiful and strange. I am in an enchanted wood following an old woman. We talk, and I can't quite hear our words, yet I understand. We visit a house in the woods, but suddenly I arrive at my great-grandfather's farm, and my family is there. I am with them for a brief time, then alone again, riding a horse, my long hair loose and whipping behind me.

The fire's stories continue uninterrupted, a journey that lasts an instant, yet all night. I wake in the morning, snug in my sleeping bag, to the smell of the coffee boiler. It is a chilly, blue-gray dawn. Dad rises to stir the coals still visible under the ashes. Nothing about this early morning seems as real as the dreams that came to me in the fire's flames.

※

It has grown late; I have been lost in fire dreams. I look around to see if my neighbors have the same dreaminess in their eyes. Several children sit still and content on laps, mesmerized by the flames' dance. Maggie climbs into my lap. Her face grows quiet and soft as she gazes at the flames, lost in her own fire dreams. Sean sleeps wrapped in a blanket next to my chair.

Maggie's hand twitches; she has fallen asleep. Dan gently lifts her from my lap and carries her inside. I excuse myself for a moment and go inside to tuck her in; when I slip her shoes off and pull the covers over her, she hardly stirs. I stroke back her hair; a few strands stick in a streak of marshmallow on her cheek. For a moment, I'm tempted to get a washcloth and scrub it off, but I want her to stay with whatever dreams the fire has brought her.

I kiss her sticky cheek, then quietly leave and close the door. Dan brings in Sean, who murmurs and opens his eyes, though I know from experience he isn't truly awake and won't remember my good-night kiss in the morning.

When we return to the bonfire, I see the quiet settling over my friends and watch the eyes of children on their laps. Rajiv, usually a dervish, is asleep, snuggled against his dad's chest. Jessica rests wide-eyed and still in her mom's lap, no longer flipping her hair and busybodying her playmates. Molly gently snores, snuggled into a blanket-lined coaster wagon. Her brother Elliott and Jessica's brothers, Kevin and Tyler, hunker down in kid-sized lawn chairs that are almost too small for them; they are quiet but not yet ready to admit they're tired.

We adults are quiet, too. Tom shifts in his seat and leans back to stretch. Jerry twists the top off yet another beer bottle and takes a drink. Sarah reaches into the bowl of popcorn. Donna scratches a mosquito bite. The talk has grown quiet, and there are lulls in the conversation, silences made comfortable by the crackling of the fire, the shifting of the logs in the pit.

The blanket my son slept on is still on the ground by my chair. I pick it up, gently shaking off the bits of bark and grass, then cover myself with it. The dew has settled, and the fire is sinking low. I glance up at the stars, then settle back to watch the red glow of the coals, the low flickers of orange and yellow flames.

Soon the neighbors will begin, one by one, to collect their kids and coolers and go home. Dan will use a stick to lift the mesh surround off the pit so he can cover and extinguish the fire. We'll go inside together, leaving the lawn chairs and beer cans until morning. As we climb into bed and pull up the covers, I will close my eyes and hope the fire's dreams, strange and beautiful, come to me.

Firebuck

Karl Elder

One antler purple and orange flames,
the other yellow, sheathed in soft blue at the base.
This I confirm with my son, straddling my knee,
authority in these matters,
since I'm a bit blind to color.
At three he thinks nothing of it,
my only failing. I love the red in his hair
like the late afternoon sun in his mother's,
I think, turning back to the fire.
And as memory makes magicians of us all,
I conjure again this animal,
its rack refueled by another log I've lain.
Now the flames flap
like wet shirttails in the wind
and I who ride
am for a moment myself,
the child content with the man he became.

Trial by Fire

Sherry Norman Horbatenko

$\mathcal{M}$y brothers, sister, and I grew up in the hills of Central Florida. Clermont was a small town nestled along with several others in an area known as the Land o' Lakes. Water sports, bonfires, campfires, neighborhood parties, and cookouts abounded.

I always knew this was where I wanted to raise my kids. We had Webelos, Cub Scouts, Boy Scouts, and all the other clubs by which we could help our children learn values and grow up to be responsible and prosperous. I married and eventually had two children, a boy and a girl.

Then I got reckless. I became a Den Mother for the Webelos, a group of six- and seven-year-old boys on their way to becoming Cub Scouts. This had its rewards, and then it had the other stuff. Den Mothers will know what I'm referring to.

We did many things: made soapbox cars, trekked through the woods looking for any manner of thing—made things, built things, flew things—camped at my house. Except for the soapbox derby cars, the boys seemed to enjoy the camping most, even though it was done during the day and in my yard, even though my small daughter was present and involved in everything.

One day was the best and the worst day of all. We practiced first aid and then made campfire dinners. You take a large piece of aluminum foil, smear butter on the shiny side of it, and place inside of it a hamburger patty, chopped scallions, and chunks of carrots, potatoes, and green beans. You then bring up the edges and fold them together several times, rolling the folded edges down until you have a mostly flat package. Then the ends are rolled upward and sealed tightly to prevent leaks. These packages were placed in the hot coals of the campfire and allowed to cook while the boys played in the sprinkler and kiddy pool.

Soon the meals were ready and we moved to the picnic table. The boys were in awe at the meal they had prepared with their own hands. It wasn't long before they'd consumed all of that and a mountain of chips and cupcakes.

It happened while we were cleaning up. I had assigned fire patrol to my son and one other boy. They knew what to do. They were to use the water hose to soak down the coals till not a wisp of smoke or steam remained and then they were to shovel dirt over what was left.

My small daughter ran out to stop them because she wanted to ask about roasting marshmallows. She miscalculated and didn't stop until she was standing in the coals, screaming and stomping her feet over and over in those red-hot coals. I snatched her up and ran for the house, where I laid her in the tub and turned cold water on her feet. She was beyond screaming now, shaking in shock, while I rinsed and rinsed the soot and ashes from her pitted burns.

I heard my neighbor's voice raised in question outside and then my son appeared at my side with pieces of aloe plants, already peeled and sliced into narrow filets. Another boy brought me an Ace bandage from the table where we'd practiced first aid. We layered her feet with the strips of aloe and then handfuls of crushed ice, all of which we wrapped with the Ace bandage. I didn't take the time to remove her wet bathing suit, just covered her in a blanket and then another one when she continued to shake violently.

My son and I took her to the hospital while our neighbor stayed with the other boys.

At the emergency room, the doctor and nurse removed the wrappings and marveled that there was no debris left in her wounds. He gave her shots for the pain, and the shaking mercifully stopped in time for me to maintain my deteriorating control. He smiled about the aloe and the ice and said it was the best thing we could have done. My son showed the doctor his Webelo badge and said, "We've been trained in fire management and first aid, sir."

While the doctor worked on my daughter's feet, he patiently listened with what seemed to be genuine interest to my son's explanations of those two subjects. My son then went on to instruct the doctor and the nurse in how to make a campfire meal.

We returned home to find the other boys gone, but the house and yard were spotless and my daughter's room was set up as a sick room. Her bedcovers were turned down and a pitcher of ice water and a glass sat on her bedside table. Grapes, each carefully plucked and rinsed, filled a small bowl there as well. Extra pillows had been added for propping her feet up, and her stuffed toys lined the side of the bed next to the wall so she'd have company in bed.

My neighbor's eyes were red from the tears she'd restrained until my den of Webelos left. She said, "They were so good. All of this was their idea."

Grass in the Footprints

Frances Derhy

Five years later:

"Isn't Nature fantastic?" muses my husband, joining me on the patio steps. "Who would have believed we could have it all back and then some?"

I put my finger to my lips. We sit arm in arm, as silent as garden gnomes. Orange-billed blackbirds hop over the lush green lawn and colorful flowerbeds. The copious winter rains have pushed up the spring bulbs into a myriad of multicolored blooms—yellow freesias, purple irises, red anemones, white narcissus, and yellow daffodils. A cloud of tiny white fragrant blossom hides the apricot tree while the branches of the lemon hangs low, like so many old men with their arms stretching to the ground, weighed down by their juice-laden fruit. The regeneration of nature is stunning to contemplate.

The day after:

Footprints in the soot. I breathe the acrid stink that follows you wherever you go until it becomes part of you, clinging to clothes, hair, and skin and filling my nostrils with black dust. I survey the damage. Black carbonized apple and plum trees. Brown singed lemon leaves and branches folded in upon themselves as though trying to escape the intense heat. Piles of sand and gravel left where the buckets melted in the inferno. Iron spade, pitchfork, rake, and other tools, but all without wooden handles. The old carpenter's bench completely gone but for all its iron handles and clamps fallen in a pile—comic if not so sad. Yellow parched lawn and dried up burnt flowers.

Total devastation. I hurt for the lost effort, the lost beauty, this part of myself, this assault on my home. After the initial reaction of shock, I fumble to keep perspective and not be ungrateful. I remember to thank God that no one was hurt.

The day itself:

It began heavy and sultry with overcast sky and hot strong wind, like walking in a convector oven, 97 degrees by midmorning and getting hotter, one of those unbearable Middle East *hamsin* days when just getting dressed makes you want to take another shower.

Toward midday, a darkening of the sky. Running up to the flat roof we see what looks like a black cloud approaching fast. Soon telephones are ringing throughout the neighborhood— Fire! We have to evacuate. Rushing grandma, clad only in her housecoat, off her bed, without even grabbing our purses, we head for the bus waiting up on the road.

I think fleetingly of my daughter's long white dress hanging in its plastic bag in the spare bedroom for her wedding in two days' time, but I stop myself. I can't let myself think about that now. The bus soon fills up, mainly with women and children, and we are driven to a neighboring village where we are treated like royalty, or at least like welcome refugees, in the local hotel. Rumors fly around as fast as the fire: this family's house has burned, that family's, then more rumors refuting those, until everyone is confused and beside themselves with anxiety.

Late in the evening the first of the men arrive at the hotel, black faced and sweaty, my husband and son among them. We hear facts for the first time. They tell us that they worked alongside the firefighters manning the hoses, jumping between the houses with fire paddles beating out flames dropped by the treacherous wind as it swirled back and forth over the area. Out of a hundred houses, one is completely gutted. Three are badly damaged. Two of these border on ours. My heart beats wildly. I search my husband's strained face, willing him to tell me straight. Sometimes breaking bad news gently is not kinder. The tense day had left me desperate for information.

"The house is OK," he finally says, "but the garden is ruined." He slumps into a chair. "The garden is completely ruined." His every spare waking minute, his much-more-than hobby, his "cave." He mourned his trees and plants but soon gave thanks for his home and family.

The ambiguous emotions lead to a new perspective—everything is relative. We had a burnt garden, but others had a burnt house and not even a chair to sit on. It reminded me of the story of the man who complained he had no shoes until he met a man who had no feet.

We had much to be thankful for. Modern-day miracles do happen and we witnessed many. The photos snapped the next morning for insurance purposes would show the black path of fire passing inches from the main gas tank. Elsewhere it led up to a door and then stopped. Several ground-floor windows had black patches directly beneath, witness to the balls of fire that fell from the sky on the crazy wind. Fire scorched the paint off the door of the day care center but didn't enter.

The pine forest encircling our village was decimated into a charred, heart-breaking moonscape: burnt stumps and twisted branches where we picked pinecones and mushrooms and picnicked in the shade. We had considered it a fair-sized forest but now we see the surrounding villages and main highway and realize how small the distances between them.

❦

I believe that everything under the heavens happens for a purpose. Nothing in nature is coincidental or wasted, although during the days following the fire, we found it difficult to find reasons for burning a beautiful forest and leaving several families virtually homeless.

Then we saw our collective spirit burst forth with a tremendous outpouring of love and care for the families whose houses had been burned. The family whose house had been completely gutted needed everything replaced in their temporary shelter—clothes, bed linen, utensils. Besides the village families who rushed to help, assistance from total strangers poured in. Nothing could compensate for the loss of a lifetime of books, photos, and personal belongings, but friends raided their photo albums for joint pictures with the family's children.

Everyone attended our daughter's wedding two days later, even those who had lost their homes. Such a gloriously happy day, just what we all needed in spite of the terrible burnt smell and the ash underfoot. We had all come through and had been brought closer together.

The well-worn cliché "count your blessings" expanded when we noticed the following summer that we had been blessed with the natural regeneration of the forest. Young pine shoots sprang up everywhere beside the charred remains of old tree trunks. In our garden, where once the ground was scorched, fresh green grass provided a cool carpet for the first toddling steps of our grandchildren.

Illumination

Patricia Hamill

*H*ave you ever found the ideal setting in which you can become completely introspective, in which to concentrate and create? Now, as I consciously call forth the image of fire, I remember all the times of reading and learning by the light of flaming logs and burning wicks.

I recall studying for college courses and exams more deeply and fruitfully while sitting by a fire, when regular light and electronic distractions of television or radio might have tormented me to give up. Of course, studying at my university's library was practical and I made use of it while I was on campus, hunching over mounds of books and occasionally greeting friends. On the days when I was home, two hours north and nestled in the woods, I studied in far different surroundings.

My parents and I lived in our cabin in upstate New York. What this small home offered in beauty and solitude, it also lacked in amenities. An older generator ran our power and we did not want to tax it into collapse. With this in mind, our evening light often came from burning mantles of Coleman lanterns or blazing logs on the hearth.

Since the only fireplace was in the living room, the stillness of these academic evenings was enhanced by my parents' stillness as they shared the same light. While the practicality of sitting close to the fire for the best light is obvious, this closeness also caused my family to remain in each other's presence longer and more often than when we lived in our other homes with easy access to electric lights in different rooms. This circumstance enabled me to ask my father for help with his expertise, history. It allowed my mother to find out what I was studying and borrow my books.

As I sat with my books in front of the fire, I wanted nothing more. The light was not all around me incidentally like lamplight affected by a careless flip of a switch; it was a concentrated light whose wood fuel I had laid and nurtured over the hours. Its glow varied, but never wavered. It yielded a soft, pulsing light that did not distort the words on my pages, but lay across them like a blanket. I felt the warmth of the flames brush against me and was aware of the darkness at the edge of my small place on the couch.

In this cocoon of light, I read and studied, focusing on nothing but the moment and the subject at hand. The flames danced and drew me only far enough away to rest my eyes or analyze a thought. The smoke settled in my clothes and smelled better to me than any perfume. The chimney stones were arranged in a careful order and fit together like numbered journals in open stacks. The colors of the flames replaced the muted tones of the books' dust jackets.

Undergraduate subjects like Roman history or Greek mythology, which did not usually hold my interest and caused me to fidget, were easier to grasp somehow in this setting. A kind of letting go of self and an embrace of intuitive understanding let the words flow to my eyes and around my head, unanalyzed and accepted. Then they settled into a practical, intellectual whole in such a way that dates, terms, and names affixed themselves accordingly.

Lengthy reads such as works by Chaucer, in Middle English with no modern translations, consumed nights that had no other obligations. There was no late movie to catch or video to watch before its due date. If someone were to sit me down and review my range of knowledge, they would find that I could recall most easily those things that I questioned, confronted, and learned in the light of this meager cabin's hearth.

It has been a number of years since we lived Upstate full time. My family and I have since moved into "normal" houses with all the amenities, using traditional lamps, overhead lighting, and all things electric. I've completed my school work and hold a master's degree, officially in Irish literature, unofficially in the art of alternative light sources and study environments, and I feel a great sense of accomplishment. We have kept the cabin, though, and I still visit it often for a strong dose of what I call the "pioneer spirit."

I spend evenings by the fire in a meditative state, sitting for hours. Sometimes I enjoy the peaceful productivity of devouring the longest, most intense read I can get my hands on. Had I not enjoyed the comfort of firelight in my scholarly pursuits, I would never have been so enriched.

The Sacred Fires of La Loba

Joan Koerper, Ph.D.

The ancient archetypal story of *La Loba* is of a Wild Woman who gathers the bones of animals. With a penchant for wolves, she chants and sings them back to life. From the first time I read Clarissa Pinkola Estes's retelling of the story, my deep psyche identified with La Loba. She became a guardian for me, a friend. I grew to see her as both an external and internal nurturing source; a guiding spirit. I realized the Wild Woman of my soul was a powerful force calling my bones to a new, fuller life.

That's why, when I saw the advertisement for a single-firing workshop at La Loba Clay Ranch in Colorado, with a potter whose work I admire, I picked up the phone and was the first to register. I had only experienced firing pottery in two stages and was anxious to learn the process of single firing, which allows greenware, or unfired pottery, to safely fire to maturity in one firing.

That summer, I spent ten days at La Loba Clay Ranch, a gorgeous forty-acre ranch in a secluded rolling valley, twelve miles south of Steamboat Springs. Three gentle horses welcomed my arrival and patiently waited as I surveyed the large bright studio and carried my baggage to the second floor bunkhouse. The ambiance created by the landscape, gracious hosts, animal souls, comfortable and inviting main house, and excellent food, inspired my artist soul.

The early morning beauty of the frost-nipped valley foreshadowed the state of the throwing clay. Stored in the barn, it was cold, hard, and unworkable for me. It was unknown clay, Western clay, surprisingly different from the Eastern clays I had learned to throw with in hot, steamy Florida. For two days I struggled in vain. Was I ever going to sing this clay to its next stage of life?

Finally, after testing and switching clays, my silent chants accompanied the rhythms of the wheel, and my hands were birthing form bit by bit, bodying forth living vessels from the now plastic clay. My forms, albeit small cups, tumblers, and bowls, were identifiable beings, shaped, altered, and trimmed.

An unexpected thrill of the pilgrimage was my first encounter with firing in a salt kiln. It completely entranced me. The salt kiln is a gas-generated kiln, but when salt is introduced into the firing process, it produces its own natural glaze on the wares and glazes the inside of the kiln as well. For the first time I was hands-on involved with the loading and firing of a gas kiln. After loading, I helped our teacher, Steven Hill, and the assistants close in the kiln's access opening by building a front "door" with bricks. Steven fired up the burners.

Later that night, just at the point when the clay bodies were reaching maturity, we introduced the salt into the kiln. With heavily gloved hands, I took my turn pouring salt onto a long, right-angle metal pole. Then I lifted it to one of the portholes in the kiln. Sliding the pole all the way to the back of the chamber, I turned it forty-five degrees toward the center of the kiln.

As the salt spilled into the kiln, volatized, and combined with the silica in the clay to form the glaze, we heard a pop! pop! pop! The pace quickened and suddenly mimicked out-of-control Ping-Pong balls hitting each other, sending the sounds of July 4 fireworks reverberating across the valley.

The volatility of the experience, however, was not confined to the salt kiln. One of the hosts at La Loba Clay Ranch, a ceramics professor, got caught up in the heat of the moment and cranked up the gas, opening the flue at the top of the kiln.

Flames shot out twenty to twenty-five feet tall. The hair on my arms was standing on end, and my face, looking up at the awesome site of the flames against the dark, wide sky, was completely open. My jaw dropped as my utterances of awe spewed forth. The fire was so alive and grand, it was as if we were signaling our presence to an unknown galaxy! My inner Wild Woman howled with joy knowing she was one of the midwives who had helped breathe life into the dancing, transforming clay.

We stood there transfixed for many minutes. I was lost in the reverence of this ritual and my union with all that is beyond. Steven finally broke the spell when he stepped forward to return the kiln gas flow to normal. He had become concerned about the effect of the increased temperature on the wares and watched the kiln carefully all night long.

When it was time to unload the kiln, we learned that even in our playful exuberance, the kiln gods had looked favorably upon us. The ancient ones who guide the uncontrollable fires of the potters' kilns, to whom we offer supplication, brought the load through intact

As my pieces gradually emerged from the kiln, I was in high spirits to see the beauty of the deep speckled-brown clay highlighted by the light semigloss salt glaze. The vessels fit solidly and comfortably in my hands. The slightly grainy texture of the fired clay contrasted with the highly polished smooth sensuous lips gently curving outward.

I shipped all my pieces home, where they are now part of the "everyday sacred" of my life and others'. The small cups grace occasions of celebration by holding organic wine. One brown, altered, oval-shaped vessel, with a rim of yellow slip and a cameo of a waterfall carved into the clay, is the pencil holder here on my desk. I've sold some pieces as well.

Listening to the guidance of La Loba led me to experience another unforgettable indigenous ancient archetype, that of transformation through fire. The clay, formed, dried, and glazed, would easily disintegrate in rain, sun, or wind. Yet, by being placed in the kiln, through a combination of fire and air, it is externally and internally transformed into a virtually indestructible piece.

Somehow, I feel, La Loba led me to pottery in the first place. She took me to that veil of time where I experience complete immersion with the energy of the first fires and communion with the ancient women who discovered pottery at least 30,000 years ago. The women transformed not only themselves and the pots they shaped, but society as a whole, because pottery allowed humans to store and carry necessities and cook in ways previously unknown.

Now, I am part of the lineage of women potters, bowing before the ancients and the kiln gods, in gratitude of my transformative journey and the everyday sacred.

La Loba blessed me with a gift beyond time. That night, at the ranch bearing her name, the shooting flames, the symphony of salt popping in the kiln, the smells, the brilliant summer night, the full moon, and the primal experience of soul, community, and transformation by fire, all combined to shape one of the most magical nights of my pottery career.

Refuge

Ann Clizer

On a Sunday in May of 1980, I discovered the aphrodisiac effect of a natural disaster. It was quite an awakening, even for a woman who had grown up a member of the "free love" generation. My discovery coincided with the awakening of a long-dormant volcano those of us who lived in the Northwest had ignored for years. On a personal level, I learned the practical application of a simple equation: intensity without equals intensity within.

When Mount Saint Helens exploded that spring, the entire northwest was privy to some part of the aftereffects, even if it was only a dusting of gray ash gathered along the roadsides on the days following the blast. A single mother living near Yakima in Washington State, I was driving to my cousin's house that day so our toddler sons could play together. Unable to see in the blinding ash storm, I took refuge at a male coworker's apartment; we didn't know each other well, since he had just come to work in my office two weeks before.

After frantically banging on doors in the building to find Craig's apartment, I staggered into his living room, carrying my terrified three-year-old son, Jeremy. "Sit with him over there for a minute," he suggested, pointing at an old-fashioned wooden rocker. He guided me toward the chair, pressing lightly against the small of my back. A shock jolted up my spine, its force making my body jerk.

I sat with my son, avoiding Craig's eyes, trying to calm myself in the maternal ritual of comforting a frightened child. Confused by my physical response to his touch, I wondered if Craig had felt the jolt too.

Maybe the charged ions from the volcano blast penetrated the apartment walls, but within minutes, there was no doubt that Craig and I were powerfully attracted to one another. Babbling about my drive through the storm, I felt Craig's eyes on me as I settled my son into his portable playpen with the toys a bachelor would have: plastic cups, a sponge, two Styrofoam egg cartons, a margarine tub, and assorted Tupperware. I added the few toys we had brought with us—some plastic army guys and two Hot Wheels cars. We left the bedroom door open and slipped around the corner onto the daybed, our lips meeting in the first exploratory kiss. Surely I was a terrible mother, but the urgency of our attraction overwhelmed me. Jeremy's little-boy narration of the cars and army guys reliving our recent adventure provided the background to our lovemaking.

It wasn't the first time I'd gone to bed with a man I barely knew, but the intensity of the experience was almost frightening. Each touch of his hand was like lava, hot to the point of burning, and waves of weakness spread downward from my lips with every kiss. I could not get enough. Outside the window, ash swirled as if the world was one of those tiny balls with winter scenes of people skating in the snow, but on the daybed, it was me doing the shaking. I was out of control, but going with the flow was my only possible choice.

Craig and I played on the bed while Jeremy played in the corner of the living room. The powerful drug of sensual pleasure, along with the urgency of my inner fire, displaced any guilt I felt about not paying attention to my son, almost obliterating my apprehension about how the volcanic eruption would affect our beautiful valley of apple orchards. Later the three of us sat on our knees around the coffee table eating the frozen dinners Craig served, watching newscasts that showed Mount Saint Helens blasting its top off over and over. Whoever taped the explosion had captured the event at incredibly close range, and the film mesmerized us. The awesome power of that blast burned its unforgettable image into my mind that night. I rocked Jeremy to sleep in the wooden chair, then laid him down on a sleeping bag in the corner. Craig and I escaped again into our nest of carnal delights.

The next morning, instead of heading off to work, it was more of the same: ashes and sex. After lunch, Jeremy was tired of the confinement, so I read *Curious George* to him half a dozen times, silently cursing myself for only packing one book. Craig and I exchanged longing looks, but our window of opportunity had closed. It wouldn't be until the next weekend that we discovered our magic had gone flat. Overpowering passion, along with volcanic ash, had sunk to ground level and refused to be rejuvenated.

By Monday afternoon, the streets of Yakima were officially open. I drove home through a drift of gray. Everything was covered in ash, and it swirled around our car with the wind of our passing. Jeremy and I stared at the dull world around us. Nature's colors were muted, with trees, flowers, lawns, and bushes camouflaged in ash. Cars were blanketed, and even the hills around the city, which had been tinged with the new life of spring green, sulked in their drab covering.

But the elements work in harmony, of course. Forgiving earth absorbed fire's offering, that rich ash blown through the air by wind and washed into gullies and ditches by rain water. When I tour the Northwest by car more than twenty years later, I can't see any trace of the eruption, though I know the flattened forest near the mountain itself will take decades to regenerate.

The fleeting grand passion that engulfed me is forever linked in memory with the image of that earth-moving blast. A still photo of the Mount Saint Helens eruption hangs on my office wall, a testament to the intense possibilities one can wake up to on any given day.

A Wedding Tale

Roberta Beach Jacobson

My friend was faced with planning her wedding and reception, and she and her boyfriend had little money to spend for either. It was quite a daunting task to plan such an event, so I suggested maybe I could help her.

We brainstormed and came up with a list of cost-cutting ideas, everything from her borrowing a gown from another friend to holding both the wedding ceremony and reception outdoors. We were on a roll and we made quite an efficient planning team—coming up with all sorts of thrifty possibilities.

The late-evening wedding ceremony was elegantly simple. It went off without a hitch and it took only about a dozen minutes. Strange, how such a momentous occasion in somebody's life could happen so quickly almost in the blink of an eye.

Wedding guests, about forty of us, gathered nearby on the wooden benches set up around a pit where a huge bonfire was roaring. It was a welcoming site, perfect for warding off the late September chill. We sipped drinks and ate spicy snacks and small sandwiches.

I can assure you this wasn't on our idea list, but the bride and groom walked hand in hand to the fire. They stood with their backs to the flames and she tossed her bouquet high into the night sky. In it went and the fire reacted with a sparkly shower of light. We clapped. We laughed. We congratulated the happy couple. None of us could ever remember any celebration quite like this before!

A fire has a way of making you stare at it and that's what we did. We were mesmerized as the red and yellow sparks shot into the air. The fire snapped and cracked irregularly, unpredictably. Sometimes we had to turn away momentarily because of its intensity.

Who needed a band? The fire was the best entertainment we could have imagined, and guests felt at ease in its presence. We chatted with one another and enjoyed the refreshments, the conversations, the mood. In the glow of the fire, old friends met up again and new friendships formed.

The groom and his father regularly fed the bonfire with cherry wood. As we watched it go up in smoke, its sweetness permeated our noses. It added another dimension to our enjoyment and I can still recapture that smell, some six years later.

To me, the evening spent around the comfort of the fire was perfect in every way. The hours slipped by and night became day. It was hard to leave to go home. How odd that for months before, my friend and I had asked each other repeatedly if guests might feel shortchanged by the outdoor offerings. Had my friend opted to hold her reception in a traditional setting, in a hall with a catering team and a band at the ready, she would have spent a year's pay, which certainly was not a viable option.

How simple life can be when we let nature take center stage.

Wedding Night

Ian McDonald

This cloudless night
stars crowd the sky,
a whirling bee-storm
glitters above the trees.
A table is alight with silver,
lustrous gifts presented
to shine with brilliant flowers.
The holy fire burns
amid murmuring of prayers.
Scarlet adorns her head,
sari of kindled flame.
Gold anklets shine on her feet
gold bracelets shine on her arms
a gold necklace gleams at her throat.
But brighter than all
burning with love
are her dark eyes
glowing in the lamplight.

The Sirens Called

Angelique Cuillierier

Broken up with the love of her life at age thirty-three, my dear friend (height 4 feet 11 inches) decided to devote herself to learning how to be a volunteer firefighter. Small though she is, she has a mighty spirit. She shaved off her abundant hair so it wouldn't get in the way (and also to make a statement about her grieving heart). She took classes and workshops, crawled through brush on her belly, helped set fire to old buildings, and practiced putting them out.

She had also survived a house fire in college and this was her way of purging the ongoing angst and uncertainty that accompanies this sort of trauma. More than that, firefighting seemed to represent a way of regaining control of her life, her passionate self laid waste. The "boyfriend" claimed he was too old for her—and at the same time had been seeing another woman closer to his age. For her part, she had given herself wholly to him and was deeply committed to the open and honest sharing of thoughts and feelings essential to a healthy relationship. She had thought he was, too.

In her new firefighting life, she was on call day and night and willingly rushed to the aid of perfect strangers. One night as she lay sleeping, her beeper went off, and she learned that a chimney fire had started at the home of her ex-lover, with whom she had not exchanged two words in more than a year. She hurried to the site and with her team got to work putting out the fire. Afterward the ex-lover and she exchanged a few kind words and she was off.

Six months later, she was awakened again by news of a fire at the same location. Again, with the team she put out the fire—this time a more serious problem. Rodents had gnawed through the electrical wiring and the building was severely damaged. After the fire was extinguished, the chief assigned her to stick around to make sure that the last smoldering remains were no longer dangerous.

Her ex—who had parted company with the "other woman" a mere two weeks after breaking up with my friend—offered her a cup of coffee, and they sat down and talked for a while. Before she went home she said, "You know, Michael, you don't have to set your house on fire to get me to come over."

Soon after that, he called and the relationship was on the mend. New avenues of communication opened up.

"I really did think I was too old for you," he said. "That's why I didn't call you. I don't want to be a burden on you."

Well, love is love, they decided. It's a gift even if he comes clad in some inappropriate garb. Certainly, it seemed that my friend's efforts to separate herself from him had actually brought them back together.

A few months later, they were engaged. The wedding day arrived and they were married in a flower-filled garden surrounding the twice-burned (and now fully restored) house.

Unnoticed during the wedding ceremony, a fire truck had quietly parked on the street. Everyone watched with tears in their eyes as the tremulous couple stood radiantly in love, exchanging vows. When the minister presented the new couple to the assembled gathering the sound of a fire siren arose, adding a memorable note to the applauding onlookers' enthusiasm.

Ten years later the only recurrent fire is their enduring love for one another.

Sacred Fire, Sacred Light

Diane Sims

Sometimes fire is disguised by light. Not necessarily the light of divine light, but by light burned bravely in understanding. It is a fire that illuminates the soul and permits the apparent darkness of death to glow gallantly.

Charlotte Mew, an English poet of the early 1900s, spilled open my soul with this stanza of her poem "Smile, Death":

Smile, Death, as you fasten the blades
    to my feet for me,

On, on let us skate past the sleeping willows
    dusted with snow,

Fast, fast down the frozen stream,
    with the moor and the road

and the vision behind,
    (Show me your face, why the eyes are kind!)

And we will not speak of life
    or believe in it or remember it as we go.

My mother was Swedish, and she treasured the hope that her body would be set adrift upon a raft with fire consuming all as the raft drifted out, awash in fire and waves, like a Viking's. She did not get her wish as we conformed to the standards of the Canadian funeral.

However, the summer after her death, friends and I constructed a fiery raft in her memory. I will never forget the bonfire we lighted on the shores of Lake Superior to forge the fire for her raft; nor will I forget the friend who crafted the crude raft. All of us waded into the rocky, cold shoreline, blue jeans rolled up and soggy, feet aching from the stony beach. We held the sides of the rough raft, as we would carry a coffin, with aching, chilled hands. We set the craft adrift and watched the glowing embers that quickly became flames. Fiery flames in my mother's memory.

It was a glorious fire and in those flames I saw the light of my mother's life. I was not the only one in tears as we watched the current take the raft into the channel. It may seem strange and sad to say, but I wished my mom was beside me as we watched the raft fade away.

Two months later, I was diagnosed with ovarian cancer, the same cancer that killed my sister, Karen, four months before our mom died. Karen was diagnosed with multiple sclerosis at the age of forty. She died when she was forty-nine. I was diagnosed with MS when I was seventeen and then with ovarian cancer when I was thirty-eight.

I am still alive. I don't know why. Sometimes I have fiery dreams of hell, and I awake with sweat. Sometimes I have loving dreams of light with my mom or my sister and bonfires on the beach, and I awake in tears.

When I was seventeen, I had to create a vision that could sustain me through multiple attacks of MS. I was told I would be bedridden at twenty-seven and dead by thirty-five. I went dancing on an all-night pub crawl with newspaper colleagues when I was twenty-seven. I was in the hospital at age thirty-five, but I was alive. I continue to survive MS, many ovarian cancer surgeries, and now a bilateral mastectomy.

I have no answers other than what I have written. Sometimes the fire is the light, sometimes the light is the fire.

Be blessed in both the fire and the light.

Candles on the Hearth

Susan Elizabeth Hale

A single candle glows bright on a winter's day. As I look out the window from my New Mexico home, Taos Mountain is covered by a white cloud. Recent snow hangs heavy on the sagebrush. This morning, each morning, I light a candle on the hearth and sing the names of the people I love.

This morning I send light to my mother, Norma Lee, alone in her nursing home bed in central California, my brother, Bill, in L.A., my husband, David, driving to work in the snow, my friend John hurting from a divorce. I sing to Marc who has moved to Florida, to Peggy grieving the loss of her mother. I sing and send light to all those named and unnamed who live in my heart, to all corners of the earth in need of a little light.

Sometimes this ritual is brief, a hurried afterthought, a candle burning in the background of my busy day.

As I look out the window on the white world outside, I'm glad for the small bit of cheer a candle brings. I remember last spring when I received a box in the mail from my brother. I knew what was inside: blue and white Royal Danish calendar plates that had hung in the kitchen of our old Victorian home.

Now here they are in my own home like ambassadors, emissaries of the past; a blue rabbit in a snowy field, an owl in a tree, a cat looking out a window, and, my favorite, palm trees and camels in an Egyptian desert. They are magic mirrors bringing reflections of family meals, my dad making orange juice in the kitchen or sleeping in his easy chair, my mother making a Sunday roast or doing a crossword puzzle on the round oak table.

After unwrapping the plates, I see something else, flashes of color. There is a smell of wax and I am back in the kitchen cleaning out drawers with my dad. I open one drawer and find it full of candles. At least eighty of them. Red, orange, yellow, moss green, ivory, lavender, and blue. Some broken. Some bent. None of them new.

My mother bought candles and lit them on Thanksgiving, Christmas, birthdays. They were used once and then snuffed out at the end of the meal, the black tips of the tapers a testament to the fact that she never let them burn all the way down. I couldn't bear to throw them away.

And now here they are: messengers from the family table, guardians of light from an old drawer getting cleaned out of a home that would be empty soon. My father with Alzheimer's was to share the same nursing home room with my mother until he died.

I had forgotten about these candles. There were so many things I didn't take that were prettier or more valuable: china, crystal, silver. I asked for calendar plates and candles, photos, colored glass from the window sill, an oak desk, my mother's jewelry, a family quilt, and a framed embroidered sampler that hung over the door saying, "No matter where I serve my guests, it seems they like my kitchen best."

Through the spring and summer, into the golden time of autumn and now into winter, I light these candles on my hearth and watch them burn. I light a candle on the anniversary of my father's death in April, one on my mother's eighty-third birthday in September. I remember hearing that the night before she went in for back surgery she invited friends over. She and my father made an elegant dinner served by candlelight. Am I lighting one of these now?

I light a candle and watch it burn. Light another. Let it go. Send light. I light a candle and go about my day. Light a candle and say a prayer. A candle for memories around the kitchen table. A candle for regret. A candle of longing for the way things used to be and never will be again. Grief and healing are like this. They take time and need to be tended again and again.

Like Hestia tending the home fires, the Vestal Virgins kindling the sacred flame, I light candles. Love is like this, a flame that needs to be watched over, a name sung on a winter's day, a moment's flickering prayer.

My Mother's Candlesticks

Charles Adés Fishman

My mother couldn't read Hebrew
but she knew the value of things
That's why she saved newspapers
until the pages turned brittle
and the newsprint broke into flakes
and why she kept old friendships burning
long after her friends were dead:
anything worth reading would speak to her
next year   and true friends would never tire
of listening   My mother loved those candlesticks
and kept them polished faithfully yet she
did not kindle their fire   Neither silver nor gold,
they had come down to her from her mother's—
from her grandmother's—hands   tarnished
pitted   the last brassy patina gone   The cups
were akilter   the wobbly bottoms would not align
but these battered objects could hold two candles
My mother knew the blessing once   far back
in her girlhood   but the flames blew out
when her mother died   These flames
that glimmer still   in Malaga   Thessaloniki
Berlin   These flames that are the ancient news
of our people   These flames that await the match
in my fingers   and the *Barukh atah* on my lips.

Meditation: Using Candles with Intention

Maril Crabtree

Using candles is a time-honored way to quiet the body and mind and prepare it for meditation. The basic idea is simple: as you focus on the flame, your mind will rid itself of other distracting thoughts, eventually allowing your focus to glide inward into "nothingness."

Candles also, of course, represent the element of fire, and lighting them can both honor that element of nature and also invoke its powerful qualities, whether they are used to release something or attract something.

Candles can help focus a specific intention. Using meditation to set an intention is also time-honored, and candles can play a significant part in bringing about that intention.

First, explore what your intention is for the meditation. You may want to do a brief meditation in silence as a way of receiving guidance for your intention. Ask your guides, your higher self, or your intuitive powers to let you know what is needed at that moment. Be ready to listen for the answer.

As an alternative, you may wish to express an intention focusing on a "thought for the day" or on something that has unfolded in a dream or in your journal writing. Be as clear and specific as you can in expressing your intention.

It may help you to write it on a slip of paper and make that piece of paper part of the meditation ritual.

Next, choose a candle or candles that will enhance or enforce your intention. Color is important (see the Meditation "Candle Colors and What They Mean" at the end of this book), but if you're in doubt about the right color to use, or don't have that color available, try infusing a white candle with your intention, since white includes all colors of the spectrum. You may also use a pendulum. If you do, state your intention and hold the pendulum over each candle color to help you choose the most effective color to carry out your intention.

Scent is optional, but it can also help you align with your intention. Consult one of the many books on aromatherapy or essential oils and herbs to choose a scent that will help create the mood or the intention that you seek. For example, if your intention is to create calm and balance, lavender- or vanilla-scented candles can assist. To dispel fatigue, choose a citrus-scented candle or a wintergreen-. Stephanie Rose Bird's book *Sticks, Stones, Roots & Bones* (Llewellyn Press, 2004) lists essential oils, herbs, and amulets you can rub onto the candle, with instructions for "anointing" or "dressing" it to create more energy around your intention.

Shape, size, and number of candles can all play a role in aligning with your intention. Choose several candles to represent intentions for a group or community. For intentions you direct to the entire world, one option is a large candle with several wicks embedded. As you light each one, visualize another part of the world being "enlightened" with your intention for peace and harmony.

If your intention involves a close relationship, choose two candles of equal size and shape, and light them both. For a family intention, choose a candle to represent each family member, and visualize their well-being as you light each one.

For an intention that you want to take place over a longer period of time, choose a tall, slender taper. Votives are also good here if lit an hour apart, so that some are always burning even if some are burned out. Place the candles together on a personal altar space, or float them in a large bowl of water.

Once you've chosen your candle, place it on your own sacred space or in a space appropriate to your intention (you might want to use feng shui principles or other symbolic means for placement). For instance, if your intention involves the heart, choose a place that is "at the heart" of your house.

Stand or sit in front of your candle and speak out loud the words of your intention. Repeat your intention as you light your candle, and see it clearly in your mind's eye. If possible, let your candle continue to burn until it has completely burned down. An alternative is to let your candle burn a few minutes, then light it again for several days at around the same time. Let the power of fire and light help you bring your intention into being.

Part III.
Fire Legacies

Stories of Fire from Other Lands,
Other Times

The Sacred Fires of Freedom

Maril Crabtree

In Guanajuato, an old colonial city nestled into the mountains of central Mexico, I found a hero of sacred fire. His name was Juan José de los Reyes Martinez, known to the people by his nickname of *El Pipila*, "The Young Turkey." He lived in the tumultuous years of Spanish occupation, in the late eighteenth and early nineteenth centuries, and his act of heroism was to set fire to a door.

Not any door, of course. The door he set ablaze with a burning torch was the main door of the Alhóndiga de Granaditas, an imposing stone fortress the Spaniards used to house military supplies and imprison Mexican insurgents. The date of his incendiary rebellion, known now as the first successful battle in Mexico's War of Independence, was September 28, 1810.

El Pipila was a miner who joined the thousands of native conspirators determined to overthrow the Spaniards and reclaim their country. Although the Mexicans who stormed the castle that day were unarmed except for sticks and stones, El Pipila's stroke of genius was to strap a large paving stone to his back to protect himself from the Spaniards' gunfire. He crawled closer and closer to the large wooden door with his fiery torch, and after smearing the door with pitch, he applied the torch and set fire to the door. The Mexicans kicked open the flame-weakened door and poured through the opening into the inner courtyard, engaging the Spaniards in hand-to-hand combat. Without El Pipila's courageous act, the Spaniards would have remained invulnerable behind the walls of the Alhóndiga.

I gaze up at El Pipila's enormous stone effigy, towering over the Jardin al Union and the Teatro Juarez, central gathering spots for people who come from all over the world to this city of culture and learning, and I reflect on the bold ferocity of his single act. For our war of independence from the British, we stormed three ships and threw boxes of imported tea overboard. For the war of independence for our Mexican neighbors, El Pipila and his followers stormed a stone castle and fought their way to a wooden door, where Pipila thrust his burning torch.

With the help of fire, El Pipila showed the Spaniards that they were not, after all, invulnerable. With the help of fire, freedom and independence became a reality, instead of a dream, for miners and farmers and villagers. Eleven hard-fought years later, Mexico finally achieved its independence from Spain.

When it comes to freedom, the power of fire knows no boundaries. In my own country, in the New York Harbor, another statue towers over an island that marks the entrance to a better life for people from all over the world. The Statue of Liberty invites those who seek freedom from oppression to come to our shores. Like El Pipila, she carries a fiery torch as the symbol for that freedom. The sacred fire of that torch burns day and night, a tribute to the passion for freedom and independence that burns in the hearts of people throughout the world.

When Fire Can Heal

Penny Ross

G randfather rolled his hands, one over the other. His long white braids and the leather fringe from his shirt never once got in the way of his conjuring. Like slow movements created by a gentle breeze, like a dance or tai chi, he picked up a handful of dried twigs and leaves and gracefully spiraled them into the flames.

They sparked and billowed into great clouds, filling the dark tepee with a fragrant haze so dense that I could hardly see Grandfather's shape. He cupped his hands, caught the smoke and flames together, and began to tumble the two elements endlessly in his hands, singing and chanting while he worked.

The room was dark except for the glow from the central fire pit. The old man sat behind me where I lay. I kept trying to turn my head to see what he was doing, but the pain in my cheek prevented me. He told me to be still and never mind him. "Breathe in the sacred smoke and make friends with the heat of the fire. Soon you will have to step into the flames."

My body slackened at the thought of this strange feat I would have to perform. I trusted Grandfather and would do as I was told. I dutifully inhaled and stared into the crackling and snapping coals. The heat, soft chanting, and noise from the fire lulled me.

As my mind fell into yet a deeper meditation, Grandfather began to speak, and as he did he slowly opened his hands. He described a blue bird no bigger than a large grape and allowed me to look at what he had molded from the smoke and fire. It was the most delicate of creatures adorned with leather tassels and beads that hung from its wings. Its color was slate blue but it glowed too with a royal blue iridescence. "He will help you with your illness, girl," he said to me. "By tomorrow you will be better with only a little rawness. The day after that you will be completely healed, but you must come back here to pay homage to fire."

With that, the bird flew right up to my nose where I had been suffering from a severe sinus infection, my cheek burning with pain. He perched himself on my face just to the side of my nose. Looking around, he seemed to be making a note of just where he was standing and at what angle he should proceed.

To my great surprise, he stuck his whole head inside my cheek and spread his wings in order to reach further. It was the strangest sensation; it didn't hurt and lasted only a few seconds. He pulled his head out along with a piece of material that looked like thin, sheer leather. As he did this, Grandfather explained that the reason for my sinus infection was that I was angry with someone, someone very close to me, and that after I properly thanked fire I could ask for more information about my anger.

The blue bird flew away with my piece of sinewy leather in its beak and placed it on a rock next to the fire pit. As soon as Grandfather told me to sleep, the fire faded to smoldering coals. The dark tepee dropped away and only the smell of smoke lingered, swirling through my mind, along with visions of being enveloped in an orange blanket, transparent and warm. I fell asleep.

Waking up the next morning was the next thing I remember; my sinuses felt raw but I was pain free for the first time in weeks.

The following evening I knew I had a duty to carry out in giving thanks. I sat in meditation with my hands in my lap, palms up, thumb and forefinger connected. Soon I was back with my grandfather in the tepee. He, too, sat on the floor with his legs folded. Again he handled the herbs like a dance—only this time, along with feeding the fire, I, too, received fragrant leaves. Some were placed in my mouth and some I was told to rub my body with. As I rubbed the mixture of oil and plant into my skin, Grandfather prepared me for my appointment.

"To show the fire that you appreciate its power, you must enter its realm, allow the flames to engulf you, and ask what it is you can give to show your appreciation of its great gift."

Fear had begun to grip me so hard that I didn't think I could move. Images of Joan of Arc came to mind, but I forced myself not to think that way. Grandfather's old voice was soothing and melodic, and perhaps the herb in my mouth calmed my terror. I felt myself, or my spirit, stand up and freely move toward the fire.

I entered the inferno but felt nothing, no pain, panic, or alarm. Instead, the fire was warm and welcoming. For some reason, I had the clarity of mind to sit once again with my legs folded and to thank the fire for having sent me the blue bird. When I asked what I could give in return, the answer came from all around me. It was quiet and not really a voice, but it grew in intensity, as did the heat. It seemed to be telling me that it was very much alive and wanted only that I respect its life and let it be known that it could heal as well as destroy.

"Your illness," the fire told me, "comes from parenting on your own. It's misplaced anger that you are feeling toward your daughter. You are angry at the amount of work she requires and that you've been left to single-handedly manage." I couldn't believe what I was being told, especially by a natural element, but the diagnosis rang true. I thanked fire again for its knowledge and generosity, letting it be known that I revered its power.

I began to stand up to leave, thinking this was the end of my obligation, but as I stretched out my legs an image began to appear before me and once again surprise overtook me. Sitting in front of me was a character that looked very much like one of Maxfield Parrish's chefs, the ones that wield overly large wooden spoons. He was long and lanky with a rubbery-looking face and a droopy handlebar mustache. He answered my question without my having to ask. "Yes, I am Fire," he said, like it was nothing unusual. A grin spread across his saggy face as he watched my eyes widen.

"But . . ."

"Yes, I know, I don't have horns and a pointy tail, and I love to bake bread when I have a few minutes."

I could feel the warmth emanating from him and felt the tease and twinkle in his eye taunt me.

"Just let them know I'm not such a bad guy. Will you?"

He shook his head in affirmation. "I am nice," he said again, still shaking his head as if to convince me. His charm and glow were irresistible, and when I smiled back he winked at me and slowly faded.

Now I was reluctant to leave and wanted to talk more, but was unsure of the consequences of my staying. I unfolded my legs and began to stand up. When I moved

I felt like I was made of liquid, not a human body made up of fluid, but a plastic bag filled with water. Was I really sloshing when I took my first step toward Grandfather? I wondered if I was going to be coming back to a solid body at all. For all I knew, I could be nothing more than embers and ash after having met face to face with fire, of all things.

I went into my daughter's room, where she slept. Young and innocent, she had no knowledge of my internal travels or the reason for them. I kissed her forehead, stroked her curly hair. As all children are to their parents, she was a perfect being. Not wanting to wake her I went to the living room, made a fire in the fireplace, and lit candles in honor of my newly found friend. I sat in gratitude as the warmth enveloped me once again.

Lighting the Lamp

Suruchi Mohan

The phone rang at 5:30 A.M. two winters ago in my home in California.

"Hello?" I jumped up in a panic.

"Your aunt wants to talk to you," said my husband's uncle from India.

"Hello?" I said again into the phone.

"Take your father-in-law away from here," Aunt said, without greeting. "You have put all responsibility for him on my shoulders. I cannot handle it."

"I'm sorry," I said, trying to sound comforting. "Are you doing all right?"

"I'm tired of taking care of him. He has made my life miserable. I am so unhappy that I have to take antidepressants."

"I know he's hard to live with."

"When I agreed to take him into my house, I thought you would share the responsibility. But now he doesn't go to the U.S. at all. I have him here all the time. You'd better come here and take him away."

I put my husband on the phone and listened while his aunt poured her anger into his ear.

"I'll come as soon as I can and make arrangements for him to live elsewhere," he said into the phone and then hung up.

"She doesn't believe me," he said to me. "She thinks we've dumped Dad on her. Apparently, the doctor thinks

Dad needs a bypass, and she made it clear that she would have nothing to do with the process."

Exhausted, my husband lay down again. I drew the curtains from the windows. It was still dark outside, but birds were waking up with a chirp. I turned off the nightlight and sat by my husband. He lay on his back, eyes closed, a deep furrow on his brow. He looked pale under the covers. I took his hand.

He felt awful, both for his aunt and his father, he said. The latter, he knew, was not easy to live with, and his aunt, who had taken good care of him, had her own medical problems.

"I feel helpless," he said softly. "I had told Dad not to sell the house in Delhi. Now there's no place for him to go." His breath came rapidly.

"We'll get through this," I whispered, rubbing his hand.

My father-in-law, eighty-two, had moved to his brother's house in a village three years ago, after selling his house in New Delhi. The village could offer no treatment for his numerous medical conditions, and now he had no place in New Delhi, where medical care was available. We had sponsored him for a green card several years ago, but after four years of coming here every year to keep it active, he had returned it to the U.S. government. With no medical insurance, it was hard to bring him here on a tourist visa. Well-to-do and homeless. That was his situation.

My husband had left his job three years ago for health reasons and though he now wanted some work, he couldn't find any in a weak economy. His diabetes sapped his strength and made him vulnerable to all kinds of infections. My own work as a writer was not yielding either clips or money. A few years ago, I, too, had left my job as a high-tech reporter to write a novel, but so far had not found an agent.

I felt my husband's hand loosen its grip on mine and saw that he had fallen asleep. I got up, went into the kitchen, and started aimlessly putting away dishes. The sun had appeared in the eastern sky and our backyard brightened up with its rays. I stared at the daffodils and thought about this latest event. Even without Aunt's call, it was hard to go cheerfully through the day. Now, I felt completely at a loss. Everything in my life had come, not to a standstill, but to a point from which events could go only downhill.

I wanted to pray. I went to the room where, on a low table, I had arranged the Hindu gods and goddesses and poured my heart out. Over the years, I had sporadically read the *Gita*, the spiritual text of the Hindus, but in my present crisis I needed something that would comfort me by relating to the reality of my life, not tell me to follow the philosophical life. As I sat talking to the gods, I noticed an old-fashioned brass lamp. I put some clarified butter in it, made a wick with cotton wool, and lit the *diya*.

Immediately, the flame threw a shadow on the wall of the darkened room. The seven-inch bronze statue of Shiva, sitting in meditation, the snakes on his body, the Ganges flowing from his hair, looked almost twice its size on the wall. I watched mesmerized: lamp, statue, shadow. I meditated on the shadow of Shiva. Although I was able to concentrate for only a few seconds, the effort helped immensely to calm me. I felt my troubles would pass, however insurmountable they looked.

After that, I lit the diya every day. Clarified butter solidified in the cold and shortened the life of the flame, so I switched to a votive candle, which burned for hours.

My father-in-law is better and living in an apartment in New Delhi, where I settled him during a trip back home.

My own life and my husband's is still a trial. We still do not know what lies ahead or how we will get through the challenges life has thrown at us. Standing tall each day is a struggle. But every morning, as I light the votive after my shower, I feel the power that comes from being able to do something about my situation. And every day, I am comforted anew by the calm, contemplative shadow of Shiva that the flame casts on the wall.

Fire Ceremony

Amethyst Wyldfyre

I sit quietly, soothed by the ancient music of the drum. Before me, the flame of a single red candle glows. I gaze deeply into its burning center. I see all that is and ever will be. I feel its heat, am entranced by its flicker. I am comforted and warmed by the glimpse of eternity that rests at its center.

Sacred fire, sacred flame, a reminder of the flames of many fires. It is evening and I am preparing to meet once more with the spirit of fire. Taking inventory. What shall be consumed this night? What will I leave behind that no longer serves my highest good? What is no longer fitting with the being that I am becoming? What should I have rid myself of long before now?

I meditate, slowing my thoughts, breathing before the small single flame before me, preparing for this sacred night beneath the fullness of Grandmother Moon, witnessed by the fires burning in the heavens, my star brothers and sisters, whose seemingly eternal flames light the canopy of the night sky.

Quiet now, I hear the still small voice within. It tells me that tonight I will release myself from the illusion of separateness, the illusion of smallness, the illusion of being less than who I truly am.

Slowly my eyes flicker open. I gaze once more at the flame before me. Lovingly, I reach for a stick, birch wood tonight. I begin to decorate it, tying on beautiful flowers and small bits of paper on which I've written my prayers for release. I begin to pray. Great Spirit, come to me now, be with me this night. *Pachamama*, sweet Mother Earth, cradle me to your bosom as I feed this piece of myself to you through your sacred and holy element of fire. Take from me, Mother, all of this heaviness, all the *hucha*, all the dross, all that no longer serves me, and transmute it for me once again. Transmute it to the light.

Slowly and evenly, I blow my prayers into my stick, my death arrow.

Now I turn to my essential oils, adding sweetness. An offering to the Mother, my prayers are blown into this oil, too, for the healing of the Mother and all her children. This, too, prepared with loving energy and intention, will be fed this night to the fire.

It is time. The darkness has fallen, the moon rises in the east. Carefully, I gather my things, the holy oil, the death arrow, my medicine bundle, matches, my rattle. I make my way out to the fire pit, where earlier in the day I arranged the wood for an easy start. A slight breeze comes from the south, lifting the hair on the back of my neck, a good omen. The fire should start quickly.

I am working in the south, working with the Winds of the South, with *Sachamama* the Great Mother/Sister serpent, she who shows us how to shed our old skin, our old behaviors, to crawl away, leaving what is dead behind.

I open sacred space. Calling in the Spirits of the Four Directions: *Sachamama* from the south; *Otorongo* from the west; *Hatunkinte*, the Apus and the Ancient Lineage, the ancestors from the north; and *Hatun Agila* and *Hatun Apuchin* from the east. Then the Spirit of *Pachamama*, she who is beneath me. I call to my sacred space, the Mother, who supports and sustains us all, the holy ground.

Finally, I look to the sky. Come Spirit, come Grandmother Moon, come Star beings, come Angels, come to my circle. Come to my fire. Come to me tonight. Be with me. Fill me with your presence and your light.

Kneeling now, from the direction of the south, I light my fire. Just as it catches, another breeze comes from the south, the breath of Spirit quickening the flames, assisting me in my work this night. I begin to chant. The oil, blessed and prayed over, is offered four times to the Mother, to the sacred fire. It is an offering of sweetness and a gift of gratitude to the four directions, a small gift for all that this sweet earth does for us.

The time has come. The fire is fully ablaze, crackling, heating my body, filling the air with the distinctive scent of wood smoke. I reach for my death arrow. Once more I whisper my prayers into it. Then I place it in the center of the burning flames. I watch as the flowers and papers curl up and burst into a mini-fire within the fire, the birch wood quickly consumed by the heat and flames.

As the last of my arrow is burnt beyond recognition, I move to the north. I bathe my body, my heart center, my belly, my crown with the cleansing smoke coming from the seeds of my own destruction. Tonight I have willingly offered to the fire my old self, to the Mother I have returned that which no longer serves, and through the fire I am cleansed and purified. Free from the past and ready to step fully and completely into my becoming.

I take up the chanting once more, staying until the last flame flickers out. Closing sacred space, I leave behind me the red embers, the remnants of sacred flames. I thank the element of fire for the magic of transformation and transmutation. The beauty and peace I feel within are indescribable. Tonight I am ONE, one with the earth, one with the stars, one with the elementals, one with all my relations, one with the fire. Tonight I will sleep well.

The Bonfire of My Mothers

Mary Ann Horn

> *Oh, do not tell the Priest our plight,*
> *Or he would call it a sin;*
> *But we have been out in the woods all night,*
> *A-conjuring Summer in!*
>
> ... Rudyard Kipling

He was at my disposal, he said, this new cousin I was meeting for the first time. Name anywhere in my ancestral homeland I wished to go, he told me. He would be delighted to accompany me. It was two days before Midsummer Night's Eve and my grandmother's spirit and I were on pilgrimage together.

The family villages! I said. I wanted to see where my grandmother was born and the river's edge where she and Grandpa courted in the moonlight.

Ivan beamed. We headed southwest out of Zagreb in his small car. Did I know that the Zumberak region of Croatia from which my grandparents had emigrated was now a national park?

"Is it that beautiful?" I exhaled my amazement. It was. Rolling green hills and valleys, vineyards, scattered red-tile-roofed cottages, small hamlets. Great Grandmother Mila's house had survived three wars and there it perched, somewhat askew atop a wine cellar, drenched in roses and geraniums. A statue of the Mother of God peeked out of the tangle. Grandma's hovering spirit must surely have been as bathed in fragrance in that moment as mine was, I thought.

After supper, I sipped wine and nibbled sweets on the lawn with relatives from three households. At dusk, ancient Uncle Franjo asked for a fire in the tumbledown outdoor bread oven. We circled our chairs and allowed ourselves to be lulled in the leap and spark of the flames. The whiff of burning oak overpowered the garden scents and merged with the pungent grapes fermenting in the cellar.

As the smoke wafted and the logs crackled, the half-hidden Mary statue turned ruby in the firelight. In that instant, my matrilineage shapeshifted within me. That quickly sketched genealogical chart my aunt gave me at the airport now morphed in my consciousness into an unbroken procession of real blood women. The procession undulated as far behind me and before me as my soul could imagine. And the ancient ruby-faced Goddess presided over us all. My genes quivered.

I asked about the Midsummer Night's Eve bonfire that would take place the day after next. Everyone fell silent. The women looked at each other, then at their tumblers of wine. I rephrased it. The St. John's Day Bonfire?

"But you will be more interested in seeing the cathedral in Zagreb," Ivan said. He proposed that I go there for St. John's feast-day mass. The liturgy would be magnificent, he assured me.

I shifted forward. They misunderstood. I wanted to see the ancient form of the bonfire on the Kupa riverbank, I explained. It was a memory from my grandmother's childhood.

Uncle Franjo said something in Croatian to Ivan and Ivan translated. "He said the bonfire is an old pagan ritual and is sinful. It is not permitted for Catholics."

Conversation stayed stalled. I did not press it.

Of course I wanted to see the cathedral—its palace and its treasury—and I did so the following morning. Cousin Marija, under whose guidance I toured that day, pointed out relics, golden chalices, brocaded vestments and—proudly—the portrait of a famous priestly ancestor of ours on the treasury wall. Maria paused, and allowed me to closely inspect it. I did. I decided the prelate resembled no one in my family.

I looked back at broad fair Marija's face, so like mine with her Slavic blue eyes, and took a chance. "I want to see St. John's Bonfire tomorrow night. Will you take me?"

The next night I sat cross-legged with Marija, her mother Jana, daughter Jelena, and even old Teta on the banks of the Kupa River. We sweltered in the blaze of a sacred ancient fire and the warmth of Uncle Franjo's plum brandy. Across the river on the other bank burned a second bonfire, and in the distance—was I imagining it?—sparks of orange dotted far hillsides.

An old woman separated herself from the happy circle dancers near us. She wore the traditional pure white linen dress with sleeves embroidered with roses. With agile grace, the woman moved through the flickering light and bestowed the blessing of touch on all around her. When she caressed my forehead, it was my grandmother's callused hand I felt.

"Devil woman," Maria said in English. The anxiety in my kinswomen's faces dissolved. In unison, with our female ancestors filling in harmony, we laughed with delight.

Maeve Prepares for Beltane

Patricia Monaghan

Before anyone praises me,

I must praise myself.

> My flaming hair.
> My noble nose.
> My brilliant eyes.

Before anyone desires me,

I must feel my own desire.

> My full soft lips.
> My swan neck.
> My full soft breasts.

Before anyone knows me,

I must know myself.

> My polished skin.
> My round belly.
> My welcoming thighs.

Before anyone loves me,

I must fully love myself.

> My briar patch.
> My secret rose.
> My fierce heart.

Before the fires blaze,

I set myself alight.

Milpa in Yucatan

Art Ritas

The bus is full of the Mayan ladies. I've been spying on them all day in Valladolid's main *zocalo*. Now, on the way to their village, they sit quietly next to their bundled, unsold goods. The narrow blacktop cuts through the scrub jungle, and I can see the smoke from the *milpa* fires in the distance. The men have been slashing the jungles with machetes, burning their little plots of land, and planting the three sisters (corn, beans, and squash).

Unlike the slash-and-burn decimation of the Brazilian rainforest, the Mayan milpa, an ancient crop-growing system based on slash-and-burn methods, does not destroy the land. The simple method has proved sustainable here for thousands of years.

First build fire; watch the jungle burn to ash; drop seeds into the hole made by the digging stick. Then the May rains will come—on time in most years—and the corn will sprout and the beanstalks wrap themselves around. The squash stands alone.

The success of the enterprise depends on the Mayan's ability to coordinate his efforts with nature's clock. The rain must come just after the planting is completed. Too soon and the fire will be extinguished before the organic material can be laid; too late and the seeds will not germinate in time for the growing season.

As the smoke in the distance rises higher, I think of this way of life as a humble conversation with nature.

We whisper our needs to the earth, plant our seeds, and wait hopefully for nature's response. Sometimes we are rebuffed by howling laughter—hurricanes and floods. Sometimes we face silence—searing sun and drought. We must return next time with greater humility and understanding, whispering again "feed us." We do not lose hope.

The smoke and the stoic expressions of the Mayan ladies tell me all this in a language that any fool can understand. I wonder, looking at my fellow passengers, if I can do what the Mayans have always done: speak to the earth; make my body a tool that works without thinking; then wait, and hope.

The bus slows for the *topes*, speed bumps laid on the blacktop in every town and hamlet in Yucatan. As I bounce, the Mayan ladies, through some trick, remain motionless in their seats. We hit a stretch where the jungle encroaches on the road. Tree limbs scratch the sides of our bus and the sound goes through me.

Then I see the flames and the curtain of smoke across the road ahead. Somehow the Mayan ladies have shut all the windows, and we're now in a tin dirigible floating into darkness. The driver never slows. We plunge in.

I am spinning. I am air bound in darkness, watching the ladies stroke their bundles of hammocks and *huipiles*. The few men on the bus grab for the machetes at their belts, and we think a collective thought: we are entering the underworld.

I am about to be born a twin, about to emerge from the womb as a herald. Mayan midwives who have borne babies in the milpa fields escort me. The men swing their weapons and open a tunnel. I emerge from the smoke following my brother, with whom I will vie eternally for the soul of the earth. Which of us is evil and which is good? Hearing no answer, we shoot out of the smoke and into jungle. The Mayan men and women stare straight ahead, impassive faces denying that we have been together in forbidden places.

Before disgorging me at the hacienda, and going on to the Mayan village of Dzitnup, the bus hits more topes. I bounce up, crack my head on the ceiling, and see my life clearly.

Back in my room, I check for the Stephens book *Incidents of Travel in Yucatan*. I find it buried under crumpled shirts in my suitcase. Opening it to Catherwood's delicate illustrations, I have hope that I, too, will be able to describe something new to the world. I will try to say that . . . like the three sisters, I am growing, rooted in a bit of black ash, the cremated, smoldering vegetation of the jungle. I will say I owe my debt to the fire.

Awakening Thunder Speaker

Greg Eric Hultman

Setting the fire fell to me by default. The first attempts at starting it were earnest, but Sacred Fire refused to rise. When I arrived, I could see that there was a problem. I thought of offering advice, but hesitated. Without being told, I simply knelt by the fire pit and began a ritual that I had taught myself as a child: starting a blaze with one match.

Although the other members of our ragtag group were all mixed blood, most had been raised in small Northern Michigan towns. These are places where the hunter ethic survives. In spite of the macho, outdoor image often projected by the locals, they possess little real woodcraft knowledge. Most are of the "cigarette lighter and charcoal starter" type of fire makers.

But this was to be a sacred fire. Sacred fires could not be made like that. A sacred fire must be raised with *deliberation and intent*. And the people of my Fire Circle knew that. Matches were OK, and that's what we used. But I would have brought my flint and steel had I known the task would fall to me. It was such a great honor to raise this fire tonight, for it was to be for the first use, or *awakening*, of the White Wolf Fire Circle of the Metis Nation's new communal drum.

I scoured my humble backyard on the south side of Ludington for wind-fallen twigs and branches, and managed to gather two handfuls of small twigs and a single dried branch that had cracked off and fallen from a neighbor's maple.

Using my pocketknife, I carefully shaved bits of papery brown bark from the dried branch onto a small shingle of wood. Once beneath that bark, I cut through the cambium and got to the heartwood, shaving strips similar to those one would slice from a carrot for a salad, until I had a pile of white shavings.

I set the shingle and the pile of shavings in the metal fire pit and, lying on my side, broke my handfuls of twigs into pieces about 3 to 6 inches long and carefully built up a kind of "twig tepee" over the shavings. I took the remains of the thick twig I had shaved and broke it up into a small pile of twigs, propped slightly above the shavings. I then laid a small log across the windward side of the fire pit.

One of our elders, a woman, offered some tobacco from her medicine bag that she passed to me, saying, "This is good." I held it while I placed a lit match under the shavings. With a hiss, the fire sprang to life, feeding on the structure Spirit had guided me to create. I sprinkled the pinch of tobacco into the growing flame and whispered gratitude.

At an earlier Fire Circle meeting, we had discussed building a drum. It was Lloyd's idea. Lloyd, our elder and founder, said, "I think it would be a good idea to build a big drum for powwow season." We all agreed.

Lloyd sought guidance from elders of other tribes and found out the proper ways for such an enormous undertaking. Blessing and smudging the materials every step of the way, he first built a sturdy frame of hardwood planks, beveled and secured to make a multisided rim about four feet across. He selected a tough, dried cowhide, which was then soaked and scraped for days. I brought one of my small rim drums and shared my knowledge of which stones to gather from the Pere Marquette River to sand the hide to the proper thickness and texture for a drumhead. The elders gratefully accepted my humbly offered information and within two weeks completed the drum.

This night, the immense drum was brought out and placed on its side near the roaring fire. As the fire's heat was drying and tightening the drumhead against the immense rim, it was first solemnly smudged. Then Lloyd passed his handmade pipe. The tobacco was rich and acrid . . . it was the true best cut of American tobacco, the kind their ancestors had once traded before it was usurped by white Europeans.

It was time for the blessing of the drum. Each elder spoke first. The things that were said that night were heartbreaking. Any outsider listening would be stunned to hear how the pain and suffering of the Native American people in the last two centuries still echoes in the life stories of the men and women around the circle tonight:

> *"Great Drum, lift your voice to the world. Speak wisdom and teach us about our ancestors and our beliefs. Please stop the New Agers who just want to take away bits and pieces of our beliefs, exploiting us just as the others have before."*

"Great Mother, we ask that you give life to the voice of Thunder Speaker this night. May she speak to my Great grandfather and his soul. He was a guy who tried to do it right but never was allowed to . . . whose land was stolen by the district attorney in 1932 because of a survey error . . . and he was an Indian."

"Great Mother, please give this drum life. Forgive my family for what they did in not following the path. Forgive them for hurting me so bad for following it. Forgive them for saying stuff like, 'Bein' an Indian is the worst thing you could ever be. Who'd want be an injun anyway.'"

"O Sacred Flame of my ancestors, please forgive us. Forgive my father for saying 'What the hell you wanta be an Indian for, they're just a bunch of drunken bums anyway.' May he come to understand my path."

As the members spoke, they stepped to the fire and dropped a pinch of tobacco. The elders brought the drum down to a horizontal position and placed it on blocks to rest its rim. Lloyd selected a stick with a matted and fur-covered head, the beater with which he would awaken the drum.

At the moment of sunset, Boooom went the drum.

"We are going to call you Thunder Speaker."

Boom again, as he found its "throat." Within moments two more elders joined in and began a rhythmic tattoo spreading out through this backwater neighborhood, like an echo from some distant past. A lump formed in my throat.

The sound was loud. Very loud. It reverberated and spread across the landscape like smoke from our fire, but faster, with great energy, a jumping, sparking spirit of life.

We were all invited to take turns on the awakened drum after that. It was no longer a dead plaything, but a powerful living symbol of our Fire Circle. Born of smoke and sacred fire, things of the earth had been molded by a man's hands into something living that spoke with a thunderous truth . . . that awakened Our People.

May the voice of this Sacred Drum speak loudly against the night. May it create sacred space in which we can find peace; a place of shelter; and protection from those things that seek to harm us.

Immutable Flame

B. A. Goodjohn

I live my life in constantly changing times. Life's flux envelops me; language constantly evolves; cave wall daubings of bison give way to galleries where dead cattle hang from wires, their hooves set in resin; fashions change at the drop of a hat . . . a wimple, a tricorn, a fedora. Even our climate lurches from ice age to melting poles.

This relentless transformation of my world is dizzying. This unending need for the new, this quest for something better, makes me yearn for the immutable. It makes me long for connection to what has gone before, to grasp one unchanging experience that links me to my past and to my future. At times like these, when I seek stability in this rushing, whirling world, I turn toward fire, pure immutable flame. Let me show you why.

Take five people from the past and hand them a tin bowl, a bundle of twigs, some dry moss. Maybe start with Richard the Lionheart, imprisoned in Austria. Sit him down on the stone flags below a blazing torch. And Queen Victoria. I'll place her in the nursery with her children. She has a tinderbox of gold, spangled with jewels from India. Take Mahatma Gandhi. Sit him at the side of a dirt road. Not the gutter, but the edge of a rice field. Make his bowl yellow. Give him tinder, too. Add Elizabeth I and Spenser, renowned poet of her realm. Let them peer through the darkness of the Queen's private chamber into each other's eyes.

Let a courtier in claret hose hold one burning flare.

Now, let's add me at my desk. Here's my bowl—red tin—and a Zippo lighter bearing a union jack.

On the count of three, imagine we each catch a spark, flip the lighter, or pull out matches, then touch flame to moss. Carefully, we pile our twigs, lean forward, blow softly across the smoldering fibers. We cup our hands: captive hands, regal hands, dust-caked hands, the entwined fingers of lovers, and my own twenty-first-century hands, then wonder in unison at the tiny spark building to flame and inhale the smoke that curls from dry tinder.

We are each enchanted, silenced, and balanced, as humankind has always been, by this essential element that roasts meat for the cave-dwelling painter and chars the artist's sweet-pepper kebabs. It warms both the milliner's medieval cottage and the Parisian atelier. In my own life, it marks the transition from the scorch of an Ionian summer to cool, soft autumn and days spent chopping wood with which to feed an evening fire.

When life becomes crazy and the instability of constant change threatens to overwhelm me, I take time to rejoice in fire's immutability. I revel in the knowledge that the flames, the cracked peppercorn aroma of smoke, the hiss and sizzle, are the same for me as they are for my five friends—the captive twelfth-century king, a regal mother in her nursery, a virgin queen and her poet, and the prophet crouching by the edge of a paddy field.

Dancing with the Elders

Diane Queen Miller

Quiet encompassed the hundred people pressed together in the ancient one-room cabin set in the middle of the earth's backbone. All that could be heard was the soft shuffling of material against material as the people settled in for the night.

The shared meal had been completed. The berry soup had been offered. In the middle of the cabin, a man knelt on a buffalo robe. In front of him were three elders talking softly to each other. Colored fabric, sweet grass, and tobacco were in neat stacks on laps and the air was perfumed with burning sweet grass.

The sacred ritual began. One by one, each person making their commitment for summer ceremony brought prayer offerings to be blessed, then returned humbly to their space on the floor.

I was seated about halfway into the room, but with each person returning to their place I found myself being moved closer and closer to the doorway. Then, I was in the doorway! Looking around for a place to sit within the group, I realized there was none.

A cool breeze was trying unsuccessfully to penetrate the hot, hushed atmosphere inside the cabin.

Pushing the door open enough to slip out into the night, I waited for my eyes to adjust to the darkness, then stepped down on the frozen ground.

Just in front of me, an old, rusted wood stove was being refilled with chips and branches, as it shot burning embers high into the night sky. A few young boys were chasing each other around the stove until an uncle told them to knock it off and not disturb the ceremony inside. The boys disappeared into the blackness near the stream and out of sight of parental eyes.

The wind had picked up and the temperature in the Rocky Mountain winter night was dropping quickly. I walked to our vehicle and found a blanket to wrap around me. In those few minutes, the winds increased, so it wasn't hard to make the decision to stay in the car. The ceremony would go on until the sun came up, with songs and prayers offered for the coming year.

The drums were going strong while the people sang, filling the clear, cold night with melodies of tribal prayer songs. The rusted wood stove was blazing hot with sparks flying through the air. Drums pounded. Voices rose in song. Wind sang all around. Snow in shades of grays and dark blues snuggled in the shadows of skeletal trees and old cabins. And then . . . it was quiet. There was no wind.

The fire in the stove was burning brightly in the darkness. There was no one close by to share its warmth. The moon was coming up behind the cabin, resting for a few moments on the edge of a ridge then slowing rising into the midnight sky filled with brilliant stars and a misty blue glow.

I hummed and sang along with the songs coming from inside the cabin. I watched the sparks from the stove float into the air, higher and higher, dancing to the beat of the drums and dipping gracefully like the fringe on a traditional woman's buckskin powwow dress.

The dignity and sense of purpose of those glowing embers in the night sky drew me to them in my spirit until I was dancing with the red and golden sparks, among the old grandmothers and grandfathers who had passed on years ago, but who come to hear the singing and help the people with their prayers. With their lives. With the struggles of living in a modern world while trying to keep the values of the old days. With no mother or no father. With the lack of trust of outsiders.

The night sing continued in the cabin. The fire never went out in the wood stove. The grandmothers and grandfathers danced joyfully in the night air until the first morning light.

When the sun was fully up, the rest of the people from our lodge circle came out, ready to break their fast and begin the two-hour drive home.

"When did you leave?" they asked me.

I shared the story about being moved to the doorway, then out the door into the night sky ceremony, outside with the wood stove and dancing embers . . . truly a sacred fire.

Red Spirit Medicine

Stephanie Rose Hunt Bird

*W*hen I think about my relationship to fire, the film *The Gods Must Be Crazy* comes to mind. If you are familiar with the film, let me answer a few questions:

1. No, I am not a Junt-wasi tribesman.
2. I've never encountered a Coke bottle falling down from the sky.
3. My story is not a zany romantic comedy, and only a small part takes place in the desert.

In my case, the gods must be crazy because they wrapped my spirit medicine in something that I spent my entire youth fearing. Its color is red, akin to a Coke bottle label. For the longest time, I had a fear of fire.

The relationship started innocently enough. I was a girl of about eight. We had recently moved from a New York suburb to a rural area in the Pine Barrens. Our house was old—I mean, really old. The foundation was covered in cobblestone, as was the fireplace inside.

One night I couldn't sleep. I came downstairs and sat down by the fire. The only sounds in the house were the settling of creaky boards, the snap, crackle, pop of the pine sap as it dripped from the logs and made contact with fierce heat, and the grandfather clock's ominous ding-dong on the cross quarters of the hour.

After a time of wrestling with my insomnia, I almost fell asleep as I nestled my small body into the arm of the overstuffed leather chair. One eye was still open enough to catch several small white objects descending the staircase. I opened the other eye, sat up, and took note. Whatever they were, they continued their descent, undeterred by my human presence. I knew it wasn't my parents. They were both black, not the pitch black of 11:45 P.M., but a warm, mellow brown just the same. The fire offered no support. Instead, it seemed to crackle and pop at the most inopportune moments, a cruel counterpoint to my anxiety. Grandfather was about to strike twelve.

I trembled, bracing for both the sounds of the clock and fire, along with the strike of the white objects, as their approach continued. I huddled there, wrapped in the cloak of mystery and fear, the fire echoing its cacophonous chorus. Finally, the being emerged. It was our black cat. All I had seen in the darkness were his four white paws.

Sometimes, just as I had thought I was seeing what I hadn't, I also heard things—disturbing things. These things can perch right at the periphery of your hearing. Are they real or imagined? We dare not pursue the answer.

Had I heard as a child that some of our relatives were burned alive, unable to leave their home in the early 1900s down in V'ginia? Could it have been that thousands of women, children, and men were burned in the infamous Salem witchhunts? How about an indelible vision of the charred remains of my people swinging after being lynched, strange fruits, according to Billy Holiday's sweet song? Somehow, something or another had seared a fear of fire into my soul that was hard to shake—for the longest time I had pyrophobia.

It wasn't until the second year of college that I gathered the courage to strike a match, and that was out of necessity. As a student potter and devotee to raku, that very fire I feared became essential. Through this spiritual Japanese glazing technique I not only rediscovered the usefulness of fire, I was able to commune with the flames and enlist their help in my creative vision. I'd fire my pot, bisque it gently with a relatively low heat, and surrender it to the red belly of the open kiln. The pot was heated to an unfathomable temperature, quickly achieving the proper glow. I'd reach with the metal tongs to bring my transformed vessel into the world.

Next, I plunged the vessel with full force into a trash bin filled with wood shavings. My scorched little pot would be quickly reduced, leaving parts completely blackened, while others had the telltale cracks that speak of raku. Those smells of smoldering red cedar and smoking clay; the intense coming together of hot and cool; the anticipation; each aspect of raku was satisfying, sensual, and too delightful to pass up—pyrophobic or not.

By the time I traveled to the Australian outback over a decade later, the dormant pyrophobia had reseeded itself. Once again, fear of fire permeated my soul. As we flew over the outback in the tiny, single engine plane driven by a bush pilot, it was apparent that on Elcho Island, our destination, fire was essential to everyday life. *Could I live with the ever-burning fires?* Through the puffy green pillows of eucalypti canopies, every few yards or so wispy gray curls of smoke from countless campfires—

known as *marri marri* in the Yolgnu language—poked through the verdancy.

Marri marri emanated from the Yolgnu's campfires amid flashes of orange, vermillion, and amber, contrasting with the aquamarine lagoons, turquoise bays, and cerulean blue skies. Having taught many color theory sessions in Beginning Painting classes at the Art Institute, I still have never seen shimmering complementary contrasts coexisting as naturally as they did on Elcho Island; the sight transcended long-held notions of the affect of light on color.

Later, as a member of the Galiwinku and Mapuru communities, I snuggled up to campfires to sample and share damper with jam (bread cooked fresh over the coals) and new friends, as stories and songs of the Marayin (the time of creation/dreamtime) licked over my consciousness.

Some of the *marri marri* cut straight through the savannah and forest. These were bush fires deliberately set by the People Who Own the Red Cloud—to clear overgrowth and encourage new production of their Bush Tucker diet (wildcrafted foods).

Setting and maintaining fires is practiced widely throughout Aboriginal Australian communities. The warming fires are revered, for not only do they assist with survival, but they are physical manifestations of the antics of the two mythical Marayin creatures who fell to Earth, bringing their lit fire sticks with them as they played their chasing games. The Marayin's abandoned fire sticks lit the dried grasses of the savannah, fanning outward to create the first bushfire. Bits of the fire were collected and have been passed on from one human to the next through the millennia.

For the Warramirri, another outback community, firelight illuminates the stage for important social activities: rites of passage, storytelling, games, songs, and dances of the creation epoch.

In a practical sense, fire offers protection from the poisonous scorpions and redback spiders, as well as a host of other dangerous reptiles and animals, since it affords clear vision of the environment once the smoke has cleared.

❦

Today, I've grown from that fearful little girl who built mystery and fear by the fire. Now, fire is a tool of healing, of surrender, passion, and desire. As I sit at my desk, a warm vanilla candle burns at my side. Now and then there is a crackle—I've studded it with whole cloves. Cloves bring energy and spark inspiration. Fire is, at its best, a tool of creativity and transformation. With this tool of the alchemists—the inspiration of fire—we can make the most valuable things out of almost nothing.

I gaze at my candle and allow the warming magic of color and scent to lick over my spirit until it has touched my soul. This little fire light at my side is indeed good medicine. Perhaps, the gods aren't crazy, after all.

Invocation

Andy Young

Kali in the bone melt.
Kali in crackle of skull.
Kali with cinder eyes,
and the blood of life
on your tongue.
We praise your purifying fire.
We praise your darkness,
the burnt black light in it,
the song of your stretched-out tongue.
Your thick flames etching blackness,
birthing blind creation.

Goddess of consummation:
Sear away the unseeing layers.
Take me beyond
this that he she me
I you true false fair foul
foe friend lover
love me beyond reason.
Make my bones sing brightly
in a sheen like steel,
the red inside the sun revealed
Kali Ma Kali Ma Kali Ma

from the fire
from the blood
from the chaos
from the flood

from the broken broken world
pull us from the ashes Kali
Ma Kali Ma
Speak through me Mother Kali
speak through this sword,
this pen that tries to praise you.

Homa Fire

Sharon Upp

Swamiji removed his shoes and entered the house smiling. Always in service of the Lord, he had arrived for our monthly Bhagavad-Gita class. A group of us gather monthly to listen to this humble teacher of great intellect give us the lessons of one of the world's oldest traditions, the Hindu philosophy of Advaita Vedanta, which teaches the nonduality of the individual soul and God. Advaita means "not two."

In the Gita, Krishna teaches Arjuna about life. The members of this class, mostly housewives of Laguna Niguel and surrounding areas, are students of life and we have been graced by profound teachers. The monks of the Rama Krishna order will go almost anywhere, it seems, where there is a devotee who wants to learn. They do this simply for the joy of being in service to the All.

We resumed with Chapter 17. Swamiji chanted the Sanskrit and we joined him. It spoke of types of worship and even of types of food and how they affect the body. One passage read, "By men desiring no fruit / Sacrifice as enjoined by the ordinance which is offered / Ought to be offered / Only thus the mind can be fixed." The goal was to make the mind *Sattvika*, or serene.

Swamiji explained that the highest form of worship was to offer the fruits of one's actions unto God. By doing that, one could be empty of desires and therefore in complete acceptance. As an example the Gita cited, "A mother who serves her baby expects no reward. She finds satisfaction in service. The good and the holy worship the Lord, expecting nothing in return. This divine act is inherent in them."

Ever practical, Hinduism gives insight into life to make it more peaceful and more meaningful. It points us in the direction of truth and release from bondage. It does require spiritual practice. What good is philosophy if we cannot live it? The scriptures provide a path for us to follow.

Swamiji explained that they performed a ritual of a *homa* fire in order to help the devotees offer the fruits of their past actions to the Lord. Mindful that the past can be a burden, I asked the question. "Can we go now?"

We were all invited to the Vedanta Temple in Hollywood, California, the next day. It was an opportunity to experience release. My friend and I agreed that it was time.

Jennifer and I got directions to Hollywood and Vine from our friend Barbara. Traveling the busy freeway, we were glad to finally see the Hollywood sign and know we were heading in the right direction.

The gentle Barbara greeted us and directed us to the temple where Swamiji was performing the *puja*, offering prayers of devotion before an altar adorned with flowers. The congregation was seated on its knees. At the conclusion, a sacred flame was held for us to take the smoke as a blessing.

The homa fire followed. In a small room with a fireplace, Swamiji knelt before a brass and copper vessel containing lengths of burning wood placed upon a bed of sand. Chanting, he offered fruit and flowers and intoned the names of Sri Rama Krishna, Swami Vivekananda, and other disciples of Sri Rama Krishna.

Jennifer and I were seated directly behind Swami on a prayer shawl laid out by Barbara. Devotees chanted Sanskrit with Swamiji. We rose and in English said a prayer together, offering the fruits of our past actions to the Lord, after which we bowed and resumed places on the floor.

The prayer went: "I who am an embodied being, endowed with intellect, life breath, and their functions, now offer up all my actions and their fruits to the fire of Brahman. No matter what I may have done, said, or thought in waking, dreaming, or in dreamless sleep with my mind, my tongue, my hands, or my other members—may all this be an offering to Brahman. I offer up myself and all that I have at the feet of Sri Ramakrishna."

Swamiji ground the ashes from the fire with oil and placed a small amount on the forehead of each devotee leaving the room. The final act was to return to the temple, bow, and offer a flower at the altar.

Even though I am painfully ignorant of the ritual aspects of Hinduism, I was profoundly moved by the experience. I felt light as air. Jennifer and I were blissfully happy as we joined others for a vegetarian lunch of delicious Indian food—rice, pappadums, curried vegetables, spinach, chutney, and halvah.

The following day, I felt a flood of emotion and love. I felt willing to forgive all grievances in the past and devote my work to service of the highest good. I felt cleansed, forgiven, and healed. Now, when my ego mind wants to pick up an old thought and run with it, I'm able to say to myself, "I gave that to the homa fire." And it helps.

Do I expect to remain in such a devotional state forever? Sadly, no. It requires a great deal more *sadhana* (practice) than that. As the homa fire is an ending, so is it a beginning.

For me, it is the beginning of more surrender and a willingness to be cleansed by the sacred principle of fire. I offer the fruits of this story unto the Lord. *Om Shanti Shanti Shanti*. Om Peace Peace Peace. Blessings to all and immense gratitude to Swamiji for all that he does for us.

Sweat Lodge

Kathleen Kirk

It was raining when we arrived, but the bonfire burned strong, heating the flat rocks we would need for the sweat lodge. Despite reassurances, I was still a bit frightened of what might happen. People had fainted, seen visions. At least we would be lightly clothed, not naked! Still, we would sweat. That was the point. To share the heat together, sweat together, cleanse ourselves as a community, and contemplate our ancestors as we wished each other well, now and in the future. It was a Native American ritual, and sharing it we would glimpse the life of a people who had tended our land and been nurtured by it long before we had arrived.

I had come with my father, who had been to a sweat lodge before. He had prayed for the health of his niece, and as keeper of the fire he had guarded the lodge entrance, opening and closing the flap for fresh rocks or fresh air as needed. He knew that rocks hot from the bonfire outside would be placed at the center of our circle inside the lodge, that our leader would ladle water onto the stones, that steam would rise with the smell of sprinkled sage, and that we would breathe an intense heat together.

I was afraid of this heat, but at first it was manageable, like a sauna. I was grateful for the absolute dark once the entrance flap was closed. Now no one would see me sweat or blush or tremble in my fear or embarrassment, should the experience prove too much for me. With my body, I memorized the position of the entrance in case I needed to escape. My limbs would have to avoid the superheated rocks at the center, so I would have to climb over my companions if I wanted out. They would understand and forgive me, I was sure, but still I hoped I could withstand the intensity of this experience.

The heat increased. Our leader beat a small drum and chanted, crushed, and sprinkled sage over the rocks, told us what he was doing at each moment, told us the stories of the Native Americans who had practiced this ritual before us. As my body grew warmer and warmer, I began to relax, the sweat pouring off me. Around the circle we went, speaking our prayers and wishes, honoring each other's silent prayers.

All I could see was the glowing of the rocks, an orangey red at the center, in a shape created by the intersection of the rocks. As I listened to the blur of voices, I let my heart move to the fiery red center, and then I was both at the center of the rocks, glowing with the intense heat, as well as at the edge as a participant. I felt no fear now, simply wonder.

Now I did not fear the blackness or the heat, even when it singed the inside of my nose, for I became a horse, and flaring my nostrils I could breathe again. I was not foaming, there was no race, though the thudding in my ears told me we were running through the mountains and valleys together, and when the soft warm drops of sweat from the horse beside me fell on my flank, like a warm rain, I was human again. My father's sweat dripping on my thigh; what a wonder, a privilege, to sit beside my father, my ancestor, in the dark, hearing of Black Elk and the directions and powers of the wind, hey, hey, hey, the sound like a mother goose gathering her goslings in a parade, and suddenly we were mother, father, brother, sister, parent, child, we were animal and human, rock and sage, we were creature and spirit. All this as I watched the glowing rocks take the shape of a horse running, then a bird in flight whose swallow tail became legs of a man, whose limbs fell away until he was but a fiery cross fading into gray stones, black space, invisible steam, our breath, the steam of us, then the water of us, then the miracle that when we emerged together, our bodies drenched, our spirits cleansed, it was still light, still raining, wind all around us, the great storm sweeping us up in its embrace.

Dancing at the Volcano

Virginia Fortner

When I was told that I was born under a fire sign, I had no idea what that meant. The explanation that my natural mode is not air, water, or earth, but expression related to all of these, sounded like some superstitious mumbo jumbo. I had learned to live mostly in my mind (air sign); what was going on in my head was expressed, often as strong opinion. That energy spent on reasoning, planning, and manipulating ideas had earned me an advanced degree.

While teaching in Hawaii, I listened to stories of Pélé, the fire goddess, and smiled as tardy students would say unapologetically, "Someone gave birth in the Pali tunnel; Pélé wasn't happy and held up traffic." To me, the goddess of fire was a convenient myth, the subject of beautiful hula stories to observe and enjoy.

One weekend on the Big Island, I sought out a black beach, hoping for a glimpse of Kiluea, the volcano reputed to be flowing in that direction. The road was roped off with yellow tape, and people cautiously lined up to watch a giant molten finger oozing down the center of the road. We smelled sulphur as it melted the yellow center line and moved slowly toward us.

I felt the excitement in a dark-skinned woman standing next to me. Her voice was musical, her frame was large but graceful under a loose-fitting *muumuu*, and the hibiscus above her ear was the same red-orange as the oozing lava. She laughed and said to anyone who would listen, "When I was a girl, we'd hear that the volcano was erupting. We'd all pile in cars and rush to where it happened. I'd wear my best dress, and I'd dance and dance on the edge of the volcano. Pretty soon, I would be so tired that I'd stop. Mama would say, 'Pélé won't like it if you don't dance.' And I'd swish my skirts and stamp my foot because I didn't want to dance, but I'd keep on dancing!"

Later, I realized she was Nona Beemer, the woman who brought knowledge of hula back into Hawaiian curricula after it had been banned for nearly a century. Once she knew I was a teacher, she invited me to join her for a tour of places changing because of volcanoes. Her stories of early celebrations of Pélé's activities caught my imagination as we drove from one geothermal hot spot to another.

Something beyond mind stirred, and warmth kindled for the magic of volcanic fire that leaves great ropes of *lapahoihoi* in cooled lava fields, shoots cinder boulders of *a-a* into the air, and changes a landscape to sharp juttings and chasms of rough lava that make you wonder if you've landed on the moon. Nona, a grandmother and mother of two musicians whose songs celebrate their island heritage, recognized the fire in herself and expressed it with grace and force.

Back at my hotel, I sat by the pool and pondered the serendipity of that magical day. The only other person by the pool spoke without introduction, telling me how his life had changed from working in an executive position on the mainland to living day-to-day in the islands. His wife had died suddenly, before they had a chance to use tickets to Hawaii. He came alone, expecting to be lonely.

To his surprise, he found himself feeling peaceful as he walked, day after day, in an area filled with huge rocks. He spoke of feeling a fire uncoil itself up his spine as he sat quietly on one of the rocks. The feeling was so compelling that he had never used his return ticket to the mainland. I listened and wondered at two strangers who shared messages about fire.

❦

When I returned from Hawaii, a friend told me that she had a spiritual experience that allowed her to give up tranquilizers. She talked about energy centers, or chakras, within her body that she consciously activated to put her in touch with divine energy. It sounded a lot like the mysterious energy the man had described beside the pool in Hawaii.

I asked to meet her guru friend, curious and trying to suspend judgment.

That day was the beginning of an ever-new journey inward for me. As we prayed, I felt my energy move from a place deep within myself, lifting upward in shivery increments until my entire body felt alive with vibration. A fire must have kindled into the flame that moved up my spine, because the next day I had flu-like symptoms. My body evidently released a great number of toxins, and I felt lighter and healthier within a few days.

I sought to return to that first stirring of fiery breath within me through daily meditation. The physical feelings ebb and flow, but a deep connection remains— with power that I can only describe as an invisible life source. It restores confidence when I don't think I'm up to meeting a deadline or leading a meeting, reassures me that I'm never alone when overcome with loneliness, and shows me innumerable examples of nature's natural cycle, which reach far beyond my frenzied activity or concern with my aging mind and body.

Insights about fire come at strange and always poignant times. I hear a fiery preacher and momentarily slip back to childhood fears of hell and brimstone, but then I remember that fire in my belly for religious values such as peace and justice can be a force for good. I build a campfire at a family reunion in the Tetons and remember the warmth of singing around Girl Scout fire circles. Those songs about the keeping of promises now mesmerize my grandsons at nap time. I hope they feel the tingly sparks of pleasure I knew as a child when my grandmother sang and tickled my face.

I back up to a friendly fireplace and feel that side get toasty while my face and front side are uncomfortably cold. We carry with us always the need to balance. The same sun that feels so good on our skin and helps the first tulip open can also beat down until we sunburn and the tulip wilts on its stem.

Recently, fire has given me a wider view of the cycle of life. I hiked the Grand Canyon rim and photographed contrasts: the few wildflowers clinging in the foreground before space dropped into vast eroded beauty. Suddenly, both sides of my path were black and bare except for skeletons of scorched, leafless trees.

Even as I smelled soot of a recent fire, my eyes noticed the canyon's muted colors becoming brighter below the contrast of the blackened rimscape. I knew from experience that, within a year, green shoots and small creatures would repopulate the area, and, within a few years, the saplings, flowers, and grasses would be taller and more dense than before the fire.

Walking out of the Grand Canyon burn area, I remembered standing above a sacred river in Katmandu on the other side of the earth. I brushed wind-driven ashes from my hair and saw a young man tending a cremation on a floating platform below. The open funeral pyre was not my practice, but I thought how the Hindu man and I both believed in a new form of life out of the ashes of death.

Fire is a sacred medium of expression, whether warming a circle of friends, connecting spiritual energy within, destroying or bringing new life. Like Nona Beemer, I want to keep dancing at the volcano's edge!

The Lantern Labyrinth

Joy Margaret Sallans

> *Fire's burning, fire's burning*
> *draw nearer, draw nearer*
> *in the gloaming, in the gloaming*
> *we'll sing and be merry*
>
> ... English Folksong

It is a still, warm evening in late August. My husband, John, and I stand at the entrance to New Edinburgh Park, where a magical celebration of light comes to life. As the curtain of dusk is drawn, the stage is set and the Lumiére Festival begins.

Friends and neighbors have gathered—adults and children of all ages—many of them dressed in Midsummer Eve garb. A pageant of fairies, pixies, elves, and little angels, with wings fluttering behind them, dance around us, their laughter mingling with the sweet music of the melodic band whose music fills the air. They each carry a softly glowing lantern—stars, pyramids, and globes, beautifully crafted from bamboo and tissue paper.

John and I join hands and follow the procession as it snakes along the path at the water's edge. A giant swan boat floats by, carrying its own brightly lit lantern. We exchange glances and my husband smiles. A medieval knight, replete in shining armor, emerges from the hedgerows and bows to us. My heart catches when John chuckles with delight. A small miracle has occurred. For the first time in many months, the sound of joy and a sense of lightness emanate from my husband.

It has been a sad year—John's brother is dying of cancer, his friend's wife dead by suicide, and both parents battling serious health problems. Death, dying, and loss have become his constant companions, and their weight has bowed a strong, vital man.

As we wander the park, John, initially reluctant to attend tonight's celebration, gazes intently at the papier-mâché sculptures of elephants, birds, mermaids, and castles ablaze with light. Live performers sprinkled throughout the grounds add to the carnival atmosphere. A childlike expression of wonder and awe illuminates John's face as he watches the scene unfold around him. Chinese dancers in colorful costumes perform at the tennis courts, while belly dancers and drummers are set up in one corner of the soccer field. Two women, named the Fire Weavers, are situated in centerfield. They gracefully manipulate flaming wands in a breathtaking performance of dance and fire artistry. My husband is captivated by the fire and instinctively draws nearer.

In Chinese astrology, John was born under the sign of the Rooster. More specifically, he is a Fire Rooster, which could explain his passionate, intense, and creative nature. But lately my proud rooster no longer struts his stuff.

John, like many men, finds it difficult to express feelings of sadness, loss, and pain. Over the past year, I have watched helpless as the love of my life has slipped into despair, denying both to himself and to me what is plain to see—his light is dying and he cannot find a way to rekindle it. Yet the magical, fiery landscape of the park has ignited a spark inside him. His eyes shine with curiosity and pleasure.

At the baseball diamond, near the park's entrance, a labyrinth has been laid out. More than 600 candle lanterns (paper bags with tea lights set inside) are arranged in a pattern known as the Seven Circuit Labyrinth. At twilight, it will be set alight and people are invited to walk the shimmering maze.

The labyrinth facilitator explains that this design is more than 400 years old and originated in Crete. One simply follows the single pathway that leads to the center of the pattern and then reverses direction on the same path to exit. Walking the labyrinth can be seen as a metaphor for the spiritual journey that brings together body, mind, and soul. As a result, it becomes a powerful tool for change and transformation. By entering into the sacred space, one leaves the secular world for the realm of the spirit. Often people come away from their walk with a sense of purpose and peace.

John volunteers to help light the candles. Armed with a barbecue lighter, he takes great pleasure in bringing the labyrinth to life. As darkness falls, each lantern glows and the magic of the pattern emerges.

"Shall we walk it?" he asks, leading me to its entrance. I feel as though we stand on the precipice of something scary and new.

As we make our way along the winding path, small children holding shining orbs run past us, squealing in rambunctious pleasure. Their parents trail after them looking harried and bemused. Others seem intent on their purpose, eager to reach the center.

"It's a bit confusing with so many people," I say. There are literally hundreds of us making the same journey tonight.

"It's all right," John answers. "Just follow the lights."

And of course it is fine. We find the center and catch our breath, gazing down the path we've traveled. With the crowd that's gathered, it will be too difficult to go back the way we've come, and though I worry momentarily that the spiritual experience might be diminished, John links hands with me, and instead of following the path back, walks us straight out. Somehow that seems fitting.

While our world feels overwhelming and sad right now, I am reminded we are not alone in this journey called life. Many others walk the same path and can help us relieve the burden of pain and grief. As John leads me out of the center of the labyrinth, in essence he is making a decision not to travel the same route he has before. He has chosen to follow his own light and bring himself out of the darkness.

Out of the ashes of death and dying, hope is born. As John and I walk once more along the water's edge, the lantern of our love lights our path.

Meditation: Rekindling the Fire

Maril Crabtree

*R*ecently I found myself confessing to a friend that I felt stressed, overworked, pushed around by lack of time, and completely without inspiration.

"I hate to admit it, but I'm feeling burned out," I said, listening to the frustration in my voice.

As I heard my words, I started laughing. Here I was, working on a book about fire, and describing my mental and emotional condition as "burned out." What's the lesson here?

I thought back to the stories that came pouring in about how fire destroys land, but nature always reclaims it. I had received stories of prairie burns and of burning off cropland, fires deliberately set in order to renew the land. Maybe feeling burned out was a prerequisite to experiencing renewal and to rekindling the creative fires within me. Instead of resisting that feeling and attempting to avoid it, maybe I needed to surrender to it and embrace it. I knew I was on the right path when I felt an immediate spark of excitement.

If you feel burned out (and who doesn't from time to time?), picture yourself as a burned-off field waiting for renewal and growth. Here are some ways to help renewal happen:

• Stop. Put space into your days. Create time for daydreaming, napping, doing nothing. "Doing nothing" is difficult for those of us who always need to be doing *something*.

• Light a candle. Stare at the flame. Sense the candle's pleasure in being consumed. Think of what passions consume you in a positive way. Make a list of those passions and look at it often. If those passions have been missing lately, think of ways to bring one or two of them back into your life.

• Take a "day off" from your normal routine. If you usually stay on the move, stay in bed and read a book. If you usually sit glued to the computer chair, take a long walk or a long bath. Try to do even little things differently—open doors and eat meals with your nondominant hand, spend time writing a few cards or letters rather than sending e-mails, skip the television news and do a crossword puzzle.

• Be curious. If you find yourself feeling stressed, act like the roving reporter and interview yourself. Stick an imaginary microphone into your brain's subconscious and ask what's stressing you and what can be done about it, both in the present and in the long term. Having a dialogue with yourself allows your subconscious to give you useful information about what will create renewal.

• Be gentle with yourself. Don't go for the "quick fix" and return to the same habits that quenched your drive and motivation. Be aware that "time" exists only in relation to our linear world, and you can create a world in which time becomes your friend, hangs out with you, lets you play when you want to play without sacrificing what needs to be done.

PART IV
The Mystery of Fire

Stories of Magic and Mystery

The Fires of Childhood

Maril Crabtree

I grew up in the city. Summers were magical because I got to spend them in the country. Once I turned school age, each summer my working parents shipped me off to youth camps in rural Tennessee and Louisiana.

My friends and I delved into country life with enthusiasm. All of outdoors became our kingdom. We played in the woods and fields from daylight to dusk, picking blackberries, creating lean-to shelters, making crowns with clover chains, and working on camp craft projects with vines, acorns, and Popsicle sticks.

Each Friday night, as the last rays of sunset faded and stars became visible, the real magic began. We came together before a huge bonfire and sang all the camp songs we could think of: the silly ones like "Kookaburra" and the softer ones like "White Coral Bells." We usually ended with "Do Lord, O Do Lord, O Do You Remember Me" or a rousing chorus of "O When the Saints Come Marching In."

As we sang, I watched the fire's bright flames dance and sparkle as if in time to the music, knowing that this magic could never be duplicated, although somehow it happened all over again each week at the next fire.

When the fire died down and the coals glowed red, the camp counselors brought out bags of marshmallows. This was what I'd been waiting for! I grabbed a wire coat hanger (there were never enough, and if you didn't end up with one you had to hunt for your own stick), stuck a marshmallow or two on the end, and began the ritual of reducing them to edible globs of white sticky stuff.

Roasting marshmallows had great appeal. I can never remember a time when I wasn't old enough to roast my own, and I reveled in the ability to create my own glorious mess. I quickly learned that I had to stick my wire low, just above the coals, and keep it turning to produce an even brown coating. I learned to be patient: if I went too low, ashes would coat my prize, or it would melt and fall off in a fiery blob, or I'd end up with a black outside and a stiff inside—not at all good on those famous dessert treats with chocolate and graham crackers. At other times, the flames licked at the marshmallow despite my best efforts, resulting in a bit of charred nothingness.

No two bonfires looked the same. No two marshmallows tasted alike. Part of the magic lay in wondering just how this particular marshmallow would turn out, and in knowing that never again would my tongue taste this very same combination of puffy and soft, crusty and sticky, white insides and brownish-black outsides.

As I grew older, I grew more practiced with my marshmallows, learning how to crook the wire into a turning handle, looking to see where the steadiest coals glowed to produce the most even heat, squatting on my haunches to watch the marshmallow sizzle and change right before my eyes.

Still, the surprise was always there, at the moment I opened my mouth and popped in the hot morsel, licking each sticky finger clean. I learned to appreciate that an unexpected flame might add a bit of crisp delight. I felt grateful for the opportunity to sit and sing around an ageless fire, regardless of how my marshmallows turned out.

Eventually I became one of the camp counselors. Now it was my turn to lay the fire, to set out the wire hangers, to make sure the new kids got their share of marshmallows, to show them how they could produce a delicious treat from their efforts.

As I watched their eyes shine in the bonfire flames, I knew they felt the same magic that I did, and that someday they'd remember the fires of their childhood with the same sense of wonder and appreciation.

Flickering Lights and Peace of Mind

Laurie Adams

It was the hardest decision I had to make in my entire life. I glanced at the people sitting with me around the table—my friend Donna, my father-in-law, my husband Jim, and the funeral director. They were all looking at me expectantly, waiting for my decision. I remember thinking, "How can I be expected to make a decision like this?" I closed my eyes and tried to figure out what he would have wanted.

I had to make the decision alone because my husband was in shock and overwhelmed by grief. Neither of us should have been forced into making this decision, but there was no avoiding it. We had lost our seventeen-year-old son to an unfortunate event beyond our control. I took a deep breath and said, "I think he should be cremated. What do you think, Jim?" He murmured his agreement and we moved on to planning our son's memorial service.

I can honestly say that I believe our son, Blair, would have wanted to be cremated. It was totally outside the realm of experience for both sides of our families' burial traditions. Putting him in a box in a hole in the ground just seemed more than I could bear. And, until that moment, neither Jim nor I had considered what we wanted for our own burials, let alone for one of our children's. I consoled myself by thinking that Blair loved summer and its heat and humidity, so this was the right choice.

❦

During the traditional viewing days, the question of cremation remained in the back of my mind. On the day of our son's memorial service, we received a confirmation about our decision for him. We set aside time for his friends to tell "Blair stories." While one of his girlfriends was speaking, the lights began to blink on and off as though someone was flicking the light switch. There was no storm causing the flickering, nor was there a short in the electrical system, as the flickering did not occur at any other time during the service.

At the time, we assumed it was a message from Blair as a general approval of how things had been arranged. This was further confirmed by many of his classmates, who came to us after the service and told us that whenever Blair entered or exited a classroom, he would flick the lights on and off a few times and announce in a loud and dramatic voice, "Ladies and Gentlemen! Blair has just left (or entered) the classroom!" They were laughing and crying as they told the story.

The most concrete confirmation came less than a week later, from a woman who had been our neighbor at the time Blair was born. I had given birth to Blair at home with a midwife. Blair's brother and sister were four and three years old at the time. I asked the neighbor, whose apartment was behind ours, to watch them when I went into labor. Our signal that the baby was born would be that Jim would flick our dining room lights on and off, so they would know when to come home to meet the new baby.

I had completely forgotten that fact in the seventeen years since his birth. She sent us a sympathy card recounting that story and saying that she felt it was very appropriate for the lights to flicker at his memorial service, since the lights had flickered at his birth.

A Fiery Love

Angelique Cuillierier

I was teaching Transcendental Meditation, and prior to instruction the teachers met and briefly interviewed each prospective initiate. When I met my first student of the day, my eyes locked in his and my heart quite literally began pounding. I almost fainted.

He was IT, the ONE. In all my thirty-six years of life I had never believed that someone could so instantly recognize and love a person on first sight, yet there it was!

As I prepared the meditation altar, I offered a prayer to the guru and also, alarmingly, I prayed to Lord Shiva, the destructive aspect of the Hindu tripartite godhead: Creation(Brahma), Preservation (Vishnu), Destruction (Shiva). Three parts of the One Creative Energy. Vishnu in the form of Krishna is often associated with romantic, passionate love.

Why wasn't my prayer to Krishna? Instead, I prayed to Shiva (also, incidentally, lord of the dance). And that prayer was, "Let me love this man and let him love me even if it destroys us both!" I wrote it down and put it behind the holy picture on the altar.

The object of my passion came in. I performed a ceremony and then taught him a mantra. After he had practiced it for a while, I asked him how he was doing.

"I was worried about the picture being on fire," he said. "But I see it's all right now, so no problem, I guess."

I looked at it—no smoke, even. He must have seen a spiritual fire, I thought—the inner fire of burning away karma with the help of an enlightened master. He closed his eyes and continued to meditate, and I with him.

After he left, I cleaned up the altar and found the charred remains of my prayer beneath the undamaged picture. No, I can't explain this—the heat of the prayer, the heat of meditation bringing about spontaneous combustion that nevertheless did not set the entire altar on fire. I keep the black-edged bits of paper in a silk bag to this day.

We married. It was a fierce though not sexual love. We destroyed big chunks of one another's egos and at the same time shared profound spiritual experiences. Lord Shiva danced on us until our bodies and our souls were pulp. We wept. We burned. We thought of ourselves as Tamino and Pamina of "The Magic Flute," going through the trials of Air, Earth, Water, and Fire. Especially Fire. In recognition of this we hiked in the desert, we participated in sweat lodges and firewalks.

And then Shiva was finished with us. My beloved came "out of the closet" and now has a rewarding and full relationship with a wonderful man. (Shiva is also the only deity I know of in the Hindu pantheon who is sometimes represented as an androgyne—half man, half woman.) After twelve years, my dearest love and I went our separate ways.

But the intuitive fire fed by that relationship still burns thirty years later. We stay in touch. We talk at length—and on occasion visit in person. Sometimes these visits are almost too hot to bear—yet we always end these times purged and renewed and terribly grateful for what we have together— an ability to share spiritual and metaphysical journeys in a unique way that is highly meaningful to us both.

A Vision of Sacred Fire

By Barbara Ardinger

It's said that one of the powers of fire is transformation. An invisible fire changed my life.

As a child, I always stayed clear across the kitchen from my grandmother's gas stove. I never knew why. It just terrified me.

When I got old enough to babysit, the family I spent most of my Saturday nights with also had a gas stove. Any time I was supposed to cook supper for the children, I was always extraordinarily careful—the pilot light had me shaking in my socks. The eight-year-old daughter was, in fact, more confident than I was in the kitchen. If the mother was going to prepare a meal ahead of time, I generally asked her to leave it in the electric crock pot.

During my teen years I went camping once or twice with the Girl Scouts. I always stayed well back from the campfire. My s'mores were always half-melted, but I ate them that way without complaint.

Until I was in my thirties, I stayed away from flames and fire. I avoided cozy fireplaces and candles. Then I fell in love with a man whose interests were metaphysical, and he introduced me to a new world. I became intrigued by psychic phenomena and learned to meditate. Hanging out with metaphysical people who had candles and incense everywhere made me sufficiently fearless, so I lit an occasional candle myself and even burned a little incense. But I never sat too close to either one.

Home alone one night, I lit my solitary candle, burned some incense in a shell, and sat down to meditate. For the first time in my life, a genuine vision came to me.

As an English major in graduate school, I had read a lot of history to put the literature in context, but I did not yet know about the Burning Times. I'd read in passing that witches were burned at the stake, but I'd never given it any thought.

In my vision, I saw myself standing on top of a pile of dry branches on a platform of some sort. I "knew" that the time was about 1600 and the place was near Paris. I (the "me" who was meditating) was looking down at the "me" who was about to be burned.

As I watched, the man with whom I was in love (and who was recognizably the same man the modern "me" loved) looked at me, frowned, and said something. I couldn't understand his words, but his disgust and fear were clear. Before I could reply (and before the "me" who was meditating could react), he turned his back and walked away.

Then someone lit the fire.

I watched myself being burned at the stake.

I felt the heat rise around me and watched in horror as the smoke curled up my body. I struggled with the chains that held me to the iron stake. Then the "me" who was meditating took a metaphorical step back and the pain vanished. I stood there (where was I standing?) and watched the burning.

I watched the skin on that other woman's feet and legs begin to blister and turn black. I watched her cough and struggle to free her hands. I heard her screaming and crying out for mercy, for help, for death. I watched her try to draw her body away from the flames reaching up to her. I watched as the rags she was wearing caught fire. I watched her cook. I watched her burn. I watched her die. Even though I was not feeling the pain of being burned, as I recall this today and write about it I am still shaken.

I don't know how long the vision lasted, only that when I came back to ordinary consciousness, my incense had turned to ash and the candle was half gone. When I phoned my boyfriend, he said, "I will never knowingly hurt you. I will never desert you." Two years later, he did turn his back and walk away from me.

I have never tried to do any research that might verify that burning. I don't need to. I have never had such a vision again. I don't need to. I burned once, in real life or in a vision, and though I felt none of the physical pain, I experienced great emotional pain.

Just a few days after that vision, I was invited to a friend's house for supper. She had a gas stove. Suddenly I heard myself offering to cook the vegetables. I was no longer afraid of fire! I'd been through it and come out the other side, and now fire didn't terrify me. Today, I light candles, though I'm always cautious about setting anything else afire. And when I decline to use incense today, it's only because I have asthma and prefer to keep breathing.

Yes, fire is transformational. My vision of fire changed a small part of my life—now I prefer cooking with gas—and a large part, for within a year or so of the vision I found the Goddess and identified myself as a witch. I know that today I do not have to go through any Burning Times.

Drawing Out the Heat

Deborah Davis

F or three days I had been sick with a fever, a tenacious, draining malady that I had dealt with by huddling in bed, napping, reading, and staring at the wall. My room was suffused with the gray light of an overcast day, and my mind seemed similarly diffuse and foggy.

Into that gray crept a tide of loneliness and self-pity. Running my hands over my body, I felt my hipbones, more prominent after hardly eating for several days. I felt the resentment that comes from being a twenty-something single woman with a fever in the middle of a long, dark Maine winter. I felt, as well, a little afraid. I had just broken up with my boyfriend. Proving to the world that I was completely independent was a thing of the past, but asking for help was still in my future. There was no one to take care of me but me. I was doing all the right things, but I felt diminished, erased by my illness. I was a pile of bones in a rank T-shirt.

Maybe on that third day I was also bored. Maybe I was fed up with the thermometer readings that wouldn't drop below 101.5 degrees and each evening climbed to 103, the endless cups of hot tea that I had to make myself, and the eerie chills that seemed to accentuate my aloneness. Maybe I'd simply had enough of Kleenex and bed rest and shivering. I had a fever, dammit, so where was the heat?

Pulling on socks, a sweater, a flannel bathrobe, and a scarf, I clambered out of bed. In the living room I reached for my large drawing pad and oil pastels. Tucking my legs under me, I sank to the floor and stared at a broad blank sheet of paper. *Drawing?* I thought. *Now? You're sick. You shouldn't be doing anything. Go back to bed.*

My first stroke across the paper brought more chills, but I kept at it. I reached for the reds, the oranges, the yellows. I pressed harder. I used greens and blues also, but off to the side, pushed to the edges of my vision. Black, yes, but only at the core, surrounded by vibrant, insistent color. I drew hard, leaning heavily onto the paper, stroking it, putting my back into it. The fever, the resentment, the aching, and a measure of fear all went onto that paper in overlapping, blending layers.

Heat began to rise in me, to permeate every cell. I started to sweat. I took off my bathrobe, my sweater, my socks. Flung away the scarf. The cool hardwood floor felt good under the soles of my bare feet. The pastels stuck to my damp palms. Moisture beaded on my warmed face. I wiped it with my sleeve.

I wasn't finished until I'd covered the entire paper with big swatches of bright color. I filled every square inch: no cool white space for me. I was hot now, and I didn't have to take my temperature to know that my fever had finally broken. I tacked the drawing on the wall by my bed, showered, and lay down for a well-earned rest, confident that I was a person of substance and fire once again.

Peyote Fire

Shumalua

It was a chilly day in March. With sixty others, I spent the day putting up the big canvas tepee and preparing the surroundings for the meeting. Someone formed a special clay altar, while others readied wood to fuel the fire the whole night, organized and prepared the food for the next day's feast, and cleaned and supplied the latrines with fresh sand. The great Arapaho roadman, Lone Star Rutherford, would be our guide.

Experienced Native American Church members carefully instructed the neophytes in how and where to sit, how to enter and leave the tepee (if necessary), what to do if someone became sick, and so on. We were told that following prayers and introductory ceremonies we would take peyote together as part of a ritual, with special sung prayers at each juncture.

The journey would be divided into four pieces and would go on from the beginning prayers until the Maiden of the Dawn brought in fresh water at daybreak. Though tired, cold, and hungry from the outset, the excitement was high. We started by passing the medicine pipe. I was unaccustomed to tobacco and my head began to spin.

The V-shaped fire crackled, giving off amazing heat. Outside, the grass bristled with frost. Inside, it was at least 100 degrees, but our backs—crowded side by side against the tepee walls—were quite cold.

The peyote was passed next. Although it was not obligatory to ingest some, the roadman encouraged us to, telling us that it would help us heal and awaken our spirit.

As we took the peyote into our systems, it began to have its effect. The water drum beat on; the songs were sung four times—the singing was both hypnotic and feverish. My face burned, my back felt like a skin of ice had been draped over it—an overwhelming nausea made me want desperately to put my head on the floor, but there was no space for that.

I sat there, praying that I would not lose consciousness, that I would be present to Spirit. Then the nausea overtook me. I vomited helplessly in front of myself. Someone came with a shovel—the waste was gone. Fresh earth put in its place. Lone Star smudged me with sage and cedar, drew a feather through various parts of my body (or so it seemed). I was given a little water to sip, some fresh mint leaves.

Once all these purifications were finished, the ceremony continued. More songs, more peyote, more drumming, more sickness (I was not the only one), more purification, more heat, more cold, more numb incoherence, more odd fright, more resignation to whatever hand the fates were dealing.

It didn't seem that I was "high"—just miserable and enduring something that in some deep part of me I believed was necessary. Each time I vomited, I had the sense that some limiting quality had been purged, that I was becoming lighter in some way.

Hours went by. I felt empty, by now indifferent to my feverish front and frozen back. An odd peace had settled over me, a sense of timelessness. I was gazing at the fire, at a six-foot-long log, narrow and turned by nature to look somewhat like a very large snake.

Ah! It wasn't a log—that was only an illusion, I now saw. It really *was* a snake. A huge one, and it was leaving the fire—heading to the opposite side of the circle. As it began to leave, the flames grew hotter, higher, making ready to burn the snake—but no—one of the flames on the snake's back transmuted into the Blessed Mother of Jesus. As sweet and beautiful a woman as anyone ever knew, the mother of us all. She held her infant in outstretched hands. "Here," she said, "my child is for you." Happiness and wonder filled my heart and soul.

Afterward I thought about this. A grueling and mysterious ceremony had—without any mental manipulation on the part of the roadman—presented me with what I had been trying to resist for years—ever since apostatizing from my Roman Catholic upbringing.

But the experience went beyond being a kind of reconciliation with what was valuable about those years of praying the rosary, memorizing catechism, worshiping the nuns who were my first spiritual teachers. It was more universal than that—and at the same time, very particular to my own journey.

The sight of Mary standing on the snake—the snake becoming Mary, through the medium of fire— that snake clearly was pure Shakti—spiritual power. This was another way of seeing the great wisdom of Shakti kundalini—represented by snake, the fire (*tapas* in Sanskrit) that purifies us so that we can see the universality of God's flame. Mary seemed to be saying that we must be burned by it in order to experience what lies within and behind the flames.

The baby was not only her child, the Christus, but was also myself, my own innocence reborn in these flames—reborn of the snake of knowledge, born of the great heat, the music—even the sickness.

The peyote ceremony was in fact a reenactment of the Great Moment of Creation. Sound, vibration, heat—the altar shaped like a great vulva, and from that vulva the fire. And from the fire the snake, the Goddess, the Child, the healing.

The ceremony marked a turning point in my creative life. With Mary in my heart, I could nurture, I could trust more fully. Her presentation of the child let me know that the fact that I had once had an abortion need not hinder me from taking a child into my heart, celebrating the child in myself, and moving forward into a form of creativity that would involve nurturing children.

These were great teachings with a great teacher. Lone Star and I spent several hours talking together the next morning and I was most blessed in this. He said he would be dying soon. He had six months to live. On August 8, his car crashed at 8 A.M. and he was killed instantly.

The Fireman at the Burning Bush

Richard Smyth

This is not just any burning bush.
It is *the* Burning Bush,
the one Moses spoke to so long ago.
This is the bush lit by the Big Bang
at the beginning of time.
This is the bush that never burns out,
that never turns to ash:
the ultimate fuel:
a small sun.
This is where the Fireman comes
to remember who he is:
a man of Fire,
one who has come to keep people warm
to share his life-giving energies.

Whole worlds arise in his wake.

The Fire Within

Roberta Gordon Silver

A revelation about fire came to me during a vacation in the '80s. Because my husband and I loved the outdoors, we chose to go to mountains or beaches whenever we needed a relaxing two weeks away from daily stress. I wanted to paint and Burt was a creative photographer. He liked to write poetry, too, so we enjoyed places that could inspire us. That's why we chose Steamboat Springs, Colorado.

After inquiring about local places of interest, we learned about natural hot springs in which some people sat in the nude. Burt, always adventurous, reacted to the information with enthusiasm. Being modest, there was no way I'd take off *my* clothes unless I had a bathing suit underneath. I extracted a promise from Burt to remain clothed, so we drove out of town a few miles and parked the car off a mountain road.

Finding a trodden path, we climbed a short distance to the confluence of two streams coming out of the rocks. One came from high above, and the other from a lower location. A few people were walking about, and others were sitting in the water. I saw varied states of dishabille, from cutoffs and undershirts to total nudity. I observed no one sitting in the higher stream or the lower one. *That was strange.*

A man lounging in the place where the two streams converged called out to me.

"Be careful! Don't get into that water!"

I stopped in my tracks and turned to look at him. He pointed above us.

"That stream comes out of a vent up there. It's boiling hot."

My mouth fell open as I saw the fine mist rising from the liquid. I hadn't noticed it because the rocks were bleached of color. It dawned on me that all the bathers congregated in one pool made by the mixing of the streams. I knelt and put my hand into the water. The water felt very hot, but not scalding. *Perfect!*

"Why is it so great right here?"

"The water from the other stream is freezing. This is where they touch."

My husband found me kneeling by the water. I explained why no one was bathing anywhere else. Before getting in, he wanted to explore the upper rocks to the mouth of the creek. I stood up to accompany him. We strolled up the mountain, respecting the power of nature more than ever.

In what seemed no time at all we had left other humans behind. The landscape became surreal. It was like being on another planet, where sky and jagged stone greeted us. Only the sound of gurgling water broke the eerie silence. We had followed the stream to a rivulet that got lost in the rocks. We noticed a thin line of steam arising from an outcrop. I could hear it hiss as we moved closer.

I planted my feet apart on a broad, flat boulder and stood still with my eyes shut. As I stood upon the solid rock, I could feel vibrations under my feet. I imagined the inside core of the earth as an inferno, swirling and popping. I sensed the heat rising upward and forcing its way out through cracks and pores. My blood seemed to surge and flow in the same rhythm. I imagined bubbles from a boiling cauldron escaping from slits in the surface. I thought how our bodies maintain a constant temperature with venting by perspiration and breathing.

It dawned on me that human bodies are similar to the earth's heating and venting system. We are made of the same elements that are in air, earth, and water. Solids change into liquid and liquid into gas, but the source of each is the same. *Different arrangements of matter, that's all.* As we require porous openings to regulate our functions, openings in the earth's surface help control the wild energy within. I had studied this in school, but before this day I'd never really understood.

I opened my eyes and searched for my husband. He had wandered away from me and stood poking at something with a stick. I couldn't see what he was doing behind a boulder until I walked over and stared. He had found the source of the stream. Steaming hot water gushed from it.

He pulled the stick out of the water and felt its wet bark. "Ow!" He dropped the stick and grabbed his fingers with his other hand.

"That burned me. Quick, I have to dip it in that cold water downstream."

I followed him downhill, leaping over rounded stones and small boulders. We scurried past the bathers to the cold creek. Burt dipped his hand into its rushing water but could only tolerate it a short time.

"Talk about extremes!"

I tested it with my hand and drew it out in amazement. "Oh! That's icy! Let's get into the part that is close to the hot creek."

We rushed to join the group of strangers lounging in Nature's hot tub. Once I settled in, I closed my eyes and rested my back against a rounded stone. Voices faded and stopped. I could hear only the rippling currents, and I felt surges of distinctly different temperatures. It varied from warm to hot, to cool and cold trickles. Scents of wet ground mingled with a faint mineral odor and the smell of my own skin. I blocked out the presence of others, discovering the joy of being alive.

I thought about fire within the earth giving life, as did the power of the sun. I reclined against the solid stone and felt the sun's heat like healing rays dancing on my arms and legs. The wind ruffled the hair on my head. I hung onto rocks on either side to avoid floating downstream.

In those few moments of intense awareness, I felt connected to the universe. I understood the concept of oneness. The earth and the sun, the oceans, the moon and tides are connected, and discrete living organisms are part of the interchange, or flow. Life-giving energy is within everything. As philosophers have said, each person is a microcosm of the universe. I felt at peace, knowing that no matter what obstacles appear before me, my inner fire, part of the earth's sacred fire, is powerful enough to surmount the most challenging.

A Volcanic Miracle

Jean M. Farber

While studying Spanish in Guanajuato, Mexico, I went on a group excursion to the Paricutin Volcano in the state of Michoacan. A seven-hour hike to the top of the volcano with younger and fitter fellow students didn't appeal to me, so I opted for a shorter hike to visit the ruins of a church in the vista of the volcano.

Paricutin, a volcano 1,345 feet high, didn't exist before 1943. A *campesino* spotted smoke coming out of the earth in his corn field and tried to cover it up. But the smoke kept coming and soon the earth began to tremble. The campesino warned his neighbors to flee just in time, as the earth parted and began spewing lava.

After a series of eruptions lasting almost ten years, an imposing volcano replaced the once flat earth. Although no one died as a direct result of the eruption, the lava from the erupting volcano demolished all in its path, including two villages and most of a fairly large church. The lava devoured the entire church except for two sides, and, as with so many wonders in Mexico, these ruins were infused with something approaching a miracle. The volcanic lava flowed right up to the altar, but did not consume it.

To get to the ruins, we rode a bus to the tiny town of Angahuan, where Spanish is the second language. *Purepecha* is the first language, one of the many indigenous languages of Mexico. We passed women in the yards of their small wooden houses, wearing hand-made *rebozos* (shawls) and scrubbing clothes in a plastic tub.

As soon as the bus parked, some twenty men, many with horses, gathered around the bus to offer themselves as guides and to rent out their horses. Most of our group rented horses or hiked to the top of the volcano. A few of us decided to hike only as far as the ruins.

Our guide was a seventy-four-year-old man who spent his days hiking back and forth to the ruins of the church. He wore *huaraches* (sandals) that barely supported his feet. He was thin and walked briskly, leaving all of us to strain to keep up with him.

We walked through quiet, lovely woods for the first part of the hike, but it became perilous as we got closer to the ruins because of the sharp rocks of hard lava that surrounded them. While I struggled up the rocky terrain, whole families passed by me—grandchildren, parents, grandparents, all hiking up to see the miracle of the altar. I was humbled to see women in their seventies, wearing stylish shoes and lovely dresses, helped generously by children or grandchildren to climb over the rocks, smiling at me as they passed.

The altar bore plants and fresh flowers as tributes to its survival. Families laughed and chatted as they moved through the rocks. It was not a solemn or grim trip, but one of affirmation for believers that the church—and the faith it offered—was more powerful than the volcanic flow.

Mysterious Fire

Rob Bosanko

His real name was Joaquin, but in the U.S. he became Mr. Jack. He was from Rio and had learned oil painting at the old opera house there. He had worked on its massive scenery, and I could picture him in the cavernous cellars with Old World visions of Carmen and Pagliacci.

But when I worked with him, it was in the New World. Paula and I had come to the Museum of the Arts in Jonesville, Arkansas, to find the roof falling down. She had said, "This is a job," so we stayed. As for me, I could see there was a stage, so I contented myself with teaching drama for children.

Soon after, Mr. Jack sent his calling card—a triptych of his work. On it was taped a card that said in flowing calligraphy, "I am coming to Jonesville, to my wife's cousin, and there will teach." When Joaquin himself appeared, he hung the three panels and announced, "The Sacred Three." I assumed he meant the Holy Trinity, but on looking I found they were Water, Earth, and Air.

"But where's the fourth?" I asked him one day as we cleaned for an exhibit.

"What fourth?" he asked.

"Fire. The fourth element."

"Ah . . . Fire is a woman and her story is too big for canvas."

"A woman?" I persisted.

He sat on a crate and sighed. "If I must tell you, I will."

"Tell on. We'll tell the boss we're researching the exhibit."

He began slowly as if drawn into old dreams, dreams that, though filtered through North American noise, were full of legend.

"Fire is a woman. It is both the woman and the fire. Some say that when Eve came from Eden she took a bit of the fire. This holy fire would never go out. But it had to be tended, and this was her lot."

"But she is also a person?" I could tell his interest was not only allegorical.

"Well, yes—I suppose."

"Who?"

"Well, she was probably . . . a contralto. When she spoke, her voice was—well, of a sort of burning amber. And she was beautiful, too. Her hair fell behind her head like a river of . . . of—well, say, splendid rust."

"Where is she now? When did you meet her?"

"Only once. At the opera house in Rio late one night. She surprised me while I worked alone. There was only a single bulb, so I had to squint to see the colors. But when she called to me, I lifted my gaze and saw her bright, true."

"What was her name?"

"I don't know. She was dressed for the part of Carmen, though I didn't realize it at first."

He told me the rest of the story:

"You there," she called. "Why are you working so late?"

"I have to finish before sunup," I answered.

She shrugged. As I painted, she stared down over my shoulder.

"You paint well," she said finally. "You know what to paint and what to leave out. Only a few strokes are needed, but each stroke must be brilliant, like lightning."

Like her, I thought.

"Señora is an artist, too?" I asked, knowing she must be a singer in the opera house.

"Don't you know me?" She seemed surprised.

"No, *scusi*, I do not. But I am happy for you to watch," and I affected a little bow.

"I have no time. I only came down to escape that conductor. He drives the tempo like a whirlwind till I scream. I came down to cool off."

"Please be my guest." I invited her to a nearby chair.

She smiled and sat.

"Someday you will paint my portrait, no?"

"If you wish."

Her smile faded.

"I do not wish. Too many lines." She touched her face. "Too much truth."

I looked up and saw she was wearing stage makeup, garish at close range. I had by now recognized her costume.

"But surely you are famous," I said, "to be playing such an important role."

She scowled.

"All women play a role, too often written by a man." Then she broke into another thought and offered some advice.

"Put more light there." She pointed to the hearth I was shading. "It needs more warmth for the children, so that the mother can cook their supper."

She laughed lightly and sat back. "I was raised around such a fire."

"And now you are a star. This is good," I suggested.

"You, my friend, are a man. So to you success is just a climb up into the tower to be king of the mountain. But for woman, there are quieter victories."

"What are they?" I asked.

"Well, my young one, they are many. To raise a family, that is one. To be loved is another. But to do either, she must entice the male."

She stood. "Carmen must be the fire to light his passion, but also the nun to keep the holy fire. She is pushed about until her frustration is a fire, too."

"This is life, no?" I said.

"Yes, true," but then she added, "Can't some homage be made to this woman? She who screams in childbirth and in passion? For through it all, she must tend God's altar. I know, for I have played this woman, I have played her till I am too old. And now I see the futility."

She looked so exhausted that I pleaded, "Señora should rest. The opera can wait." I paused, but she didn't reply.

"Is there something I could get for you? Some water? Perhaps you should return home? Is there anyone to take care of you?"

She made answer to none of this, so I thought perhaps I should see her there myself and asked, "Where do you live?"

She just shook her head but seemed to revive.

"You know where I would like to live?"

"Where?"

"I would like to live in a place where God is king, where God is fire, and we need merely breathe to feel His love. There, woman and man can live free, with no games. There, in the fire of that eternal sunlight, is Eden."

The door to the cellar squealed and three other painters came clomping down. They were joking crudely about chorus girls. I saw the cellar window showed a bit of red, but my lady was gone.

"Did you see that woman?" I asked them.

"What woman?" one answered.

"The one who plays Carmen."

Two of them looked at each other. The other nodded.

"He has seen Maria."

"Maria?" I asked.

The one called Antonio knew everything. "Others have seen her, or say so. Some even younger than you." They liked to call me "the boy."

"But who is she?"

"A ghost. Better to find a real woman." How they then enjoyed my discomfort.

"I don't believe you."

"It's true," said Antonio, painting. "Some say she was killed in this opera house when someone used a real knife instead of a prop. Others say this place is built on an old Portuguese cemetery and she was a count's mistress. But you know what I think?"

"What?" I asked, bracing for ridicule.

"I think she is a dream when one is drunk." Here they laughed outright.

"Get to work!" I countered. "This goes up in two days."

"As if we didn't know, little man," Juan taunted. "As if we didn't know *Pagliacci* opens on Friday."

"Then this is not for *Carmen*?" I asked.

"No, it is for the sad clown who is so like you." They scoffed at me once more before I waved them away and they left.

Mr. Jack looked at me as he finished his story.

"And do you know what I think, my American friend? Perhaps all of us men play the fool. Why should we try and contain the fire? Women should be free to be themselves and to be loved by us as well. Yes, for then they will be the most lovely and most passionate of all."

He took his pocket watch from his vest and looked at it, then said, "I must go home. Maria is waiting."

I appreciated my wife more after that story and looked for ways to show it. Perhaps I appreciated all women more. I was learning, and Mr. Jack's story strengthened what I knew. I was gaining some knowledge of Eve, and if not of the sacredness, at least a little of the eternal loneliness, perhaps even of the pain, of her mysterious fire.

Fire Flies

Julie Ann Shapiro

I could say I've leaped over hot coals, jumped across a fire pit on the beach, swallowed a sword of flames, and tell you I still believe in Puff the Magic Dragon, but all of these things are lies, except one. Puff the Magic Dragon still lives; he's the one (or maybe it's a she) who makes flames dance on the wings of wind.

I have lived all my life with Puff's fire brewing beside me, bearing witness to more pink smoke-filled skylines than I care to admit to; they've painted the landscape of my youth and adulthood living in Southern California.

Hearing the familiar sirens, my heart beats fast, my pulse quickens. These fires stewing in the day and night feed on a hot, dry wind; in the horizon, far from where I live, the flames have coated the sky with a blanket, making it look like a bashful sunset, while, miles away, I have remained safe. Walking outside, I've tasted the wind breathing fire, coughed, felt tears coming to my eyes, and worried that the clear blue skies disappeared and the world had turned to ash.

What these fires haven't done is paint my soul, not like the fireflies of my childhood.

Spending the summers in Georgia with my cousins, sitting on the back porch listening to the crickets, smelling the heavy scent of pine, watching the clouds hovering with impending rain, I watched the fireflies, mesmerized by the little sparks of light, not understanding how a bug could breathe fire, could be fire itself.

Wanting to know why, I cupped my hands together, arching my arms in front of my body, keeping them parallel to my feet. Slowly I moved forward above a spark of fire flying inches from my hands. I felt the wings flutter against my fingers and closed my hands just enough so the firefly wouldn't escape. Peeking inside my palms, I watched the firefly flicker. My hands glowed with each spark the firefly made. Still, I didn't see how it made fire.

Placing the firefly in an old mayonnaise jar, I watched it all night till my eyes could no longer stay open. In the morning, the firefly was gone.

I could tell you it was magic, how a flame can't be captured—only the memories can. These things are true. I could tell you my cousins let the firefly free when I was sleeping; this may be the truth. I could tell you it died and disappeared into thin air. It might be true, for on the wings of imagination the firefly is born.

I don't know what became of the firefly in the mayonnaise jar. I think it's in the same place where lost childhood is, the place between a spark of light and darkness.

Fireflies

Maureen Tolman Flannery

This is our evening ritual,
after supper, before bed,
to put a chenille throw rug
and a feather pillow
in the rusty Radio Flyer,
lay our toddler snugly
and walk west on the black top
toward maturing corn
that waves its tassels
in a strip of red-orange sky,
just walk without interrupting
the crickets or the baby's babbling
or, flashing their tiny torches
just above the bean field,
the fireflies, soon to join
their home-bound cousins,
the fixed stars
in the night sky.

A Flame of Connection

Ola Szeleczky

My father and I had never been close. We were both stubborn and had strong opinions. I felt overpowered by him and spent most of my life reacting by doing the opposite of what he wanted me to do.

Despite our differences, I never doubted his love for me. It was simply that it never came in a form acceptable to me. Although ours could never be called a harmonious relationship, we grew to accept each other and silently agreed to disagree.

My father had a hard life. Born in Ukraine, he became a refugee during World War II. After many hardships, he migrated to Australia with his wife and four young children, all under the age of five (I was the oldest). He had to work for the government for two years to repay his passage costs. He was given no choice where he would work, and despite the fact that he was a fully qualified architect and engineer he did manual labor in a limestone quarry.

Our first home was primitive, with no electricity or running water. He finally obtained the necessary qualifications to practice his profession in his adopted country, and slowly things improved. Eventually, he built a family home for us and his parents, who followed him to the new land. We were proud of him, but with eight people to feed it was never easy. He missed his homeland

and never fully felt at home. Perhaps that was why he began searching spiritually.

He tried yoga and acquainted himself with many esoteric subjects. An intelligent man with an inquiring mind, he was fascinated by mysteries and would stubbornly pursue something until he found an answer. He explored mysticism, natural health, secret societies, and theosophy.

Toward the end of his life, stress took its toll and he suffered from angina. I accompanied him on middle-of-the-night ambulance trips. Our relationship began to change. I sat long hours with him and we finally began to talk. I heard about his childhood, about his hopes and disappointments, and his innermost thoughts on many things that had interested and frustrated him. I began to understand my father.

About the time of his quadruple bypass heart operation I, too, went through a severe health crisis. I discovered I had cancer for the second time. We began to talk about death and the survival of the spirit.

In our discussions, my father and I appeared to see life from different perspectives, but now we accepted these differences without trying to change each other. Nevertheless, my father always wanted proof.

One day I said to him, "Dad, if you die before me and you are conscious, let me know. Give me a sign." He agreed to do so.

Dad survived his bypass operation and I survived my cancer crisis. We both mellowed somewhat and began to see ourselves in the other. In spite of his mellowing, he remained proud and independent and would not allow me to do anything for him. He was afraid of becoming dependent. He saw that as a sign that the end was near, and he was afraid of death. He did not really believe in an afterlife.

One day, to my surprise, he phoned and asked me to drive him to the cemetery where his parents were buried. He wanted to put flowers on their grave. It was a lengthy trip, and, at eighty-four, he did not feel comfortable driving himself.

There was a softness in his voice I had never heard before. He agreed to be at my house at 8 A.M. and said he would bring a chair that he had finished making for me.

I was delighted to be able to do something for him and thrilled that he had asked me. Although I had a previous arrangement to meet a girlfriend for lunch, I rang her up and cancelled.

"Dad has never asked me to do anything for him before," I told her. "He is so fiercely independent. I can't let him down. He was so gentle with me. It feels like we have a whole new relationship after a stormy fifty-six years."

The next morning I woke early and got ready. My father didn't like to be kept waiting. But eight o'clock came and went. By 8:15 he still hadn't arrived. I felt anxious.

I said to my son, Jason, "I'm very worried that Dad hasn't arrived. I feel something has happened to him."

"What do you think has happened?" Jason asked.

"I think he's dead." I replied.

"Oh, Mum! Why would you think that?" said Jason.

"Because I feel it." I answered. And all of a sudden, I just knew.

I drove to my father's house. I couldn't get there fast enough, praying all the way. Yes, it was true. I found him on the bathroom floor. Near the door was the chair he had made for me. It was a terrible shock.

Somehow, I got through all the formalities and organized the funeral, but later I felt cheated. I felt robbed of what had promised to be a beautiful day together.

When I finally got home that night, I lit a large candle beside a photograph of my father and sat on the chair he had made for me, watching the flame. I thought about how we had both been stubborn and at loggerheads for most of our lives, feeling grateful that our relationship had been healed before it was too late. He died getting ready to go out with me, and he was going to bring me the chair he had made for me. I knew he loved me deeply and I felt loved.

Exhausted, I eventually went to bed. I was awakened by a strong cooking smell. Still emotionally spent, I felt cross with my Italian neighbors for cooking so early in the morning.

Groggy with sleep, I got up to close the living room window, which was closest to their fence, when I saw that the window wasn't open. As I became more alert, I realized that the cooking smell was not in the living room. It was only in my bedroom, and it was a *particular* smell, that of fried potatoes in olive oil. My father loved to make this dish.

I rushed back to my bedroom. The smell was very strong. I checked the living room, where the candle beside my father's photograph was still burning, and there was no smell there. Suddenly I remembered my conversation with my father. I said to myself, "Dad, is that you?" and the candle flame danced madly.

"Oh, Dad, is it really you?"

The flame *instantly* became still. Excited, I wanted to be sure and I asked him to repeat the performance. He did. There was no wind or source of air moving in the house, and the windows were closed. The flame flickered strongly for a while and again became instantly still. My father had come to let me know that he still lived and he loved me enough to come and reassure me. I felt blessed.

The funeral was lovely and people were very kind, but I knew that the box that was lowered into the ground did not contain *him*. It only contained his worn-out body, like the clothes that we discard when we are finished with them.

Most importantly, I know that the love we feel for each other lives beyond the grave.

Kimono Aglow

Hualani Janice Mark

For as long as I can remember, my life has been a journey through the mystery of fire of the divine. When I look back on the various experiences with fire, I know now that Sacred Fire was preparing me for this one particular event. The veil that fogged my vision of the future was a kind act, for I don't know what I would have done had I known what was coming.

One evening, I was preparing for meditation, just as I do most nights. It was winter, very cold with a great deal of snow. I opened the sliding doors to the bedroom balcony just enough to allow fresh air into the room without setting the candle flames bouncing into a frenzied dance.

The house was quiet and I had changed into a comfortable bright red kimono with contrasting details of cherry blossom branches trailing across the fabric. My candles needed lighting before I sat down to enter the silence, so I began to fill the room with their warm glow.

Bless the candle, bless the flame. Light the match. Offer the flame to the candle, and the wick receives the invitation with ease. Oh look, the flame *leaps* from the candle onto the arm of my kimono! Wow, this is amazing—the flame is growing and dancing in a very particular pattern on my kimono sleeve!

I thought, "This is an awesome sight and I know that I should be jumping up and down, yelling or something." But I wasn't. I watched this glorious display without attachment and without pain. The flames' grace was kind and demanded no burning flesh. In fact, there was no sensation, no smoke, and no odor!

Suddenly, my awareness was motioned into action. My angels were likely the ones jumping up and down by this time, chanting a song of water, or proclaiming a rowdy chorus from the flaming fool prelude. I looked at the snow that had accumulated on the balcony and thought, "Perfect. There's the place to put this fire out." I calmly removed my kimono from my naked body and placed the garment in the white snow.

Kneeling down at the door's edge, I felt the cold wind. Perhaps the breeze was a sigh of relief from the angelic realm! I watched the flame, which was now ablaze, burn itself out on the surface of white. I thanked the flame for its tenderness and for the teaching of precipitation. I thanked my angels for their loving protection and thanked the masters, who were likely having a cosmic laugh right about now!

For months following, I experienced vivid dreams and visions of being led by monks through rings of fire set ablaze on temple floors. It was clearly an initiation of fire, both in the material and the intangible realms. In my willingness to walk through the circles of living flame, I gained entry into mystery chambers of great wonder—the likes of which have brought profound fullness, wisdom, and fertility to my life, even to this day.

The flame speaks to each of us in many creative ways. For me, love is a fire! It will most certainly blaze through our static position on the prevailing belief structure, and it will quite possibly come knocking at the door, metaphorically speaking, of course, if we've been caught in inertia for any length of time. The sacred fire is the beloved companion of the fertile ground of being, for it knows the language of our heart. If we accept this luminous invitation, the flame will teach us of that sweet spot, the bridge between the seen and the unseen, just as twilight is aglow upon the earth. If you listen with great depth, the flame of a candle will whisper a secret that is for you and you alone to hear.

The Eve of Hope

Bernadette Stankard

*T*he sirens weren't part of my dream. I sat up and realized the sound was coming closer. What was more unusual, bright light streamed through my bedroom window. I walked over and looked out. Flames as tall as trees shot up from a nearby roof. The roof collapsed under the fire's voracious appetite. Everywhere I looked, more flames moved in pursuit of satiating hunger. My throat closed more from fear than from smoke. I saw people running, screaming; others carried what appeared to be sticks, smashing windows and doors the fire had not yet consumed. The screams echoed up and down the street. I realized I was witnessing a riot.

It wasn't unexpected, but knowing that the unrest of the past months had built to such a feverish pitch didn't make the scene of chaos any less frightening. People used fire and weapons to destroy the only things they had, the only places they called home, because they were angry— angry over the segregation, angry over the unfairness of so many of their own being killed in a war thousands of miles away, angry because they had let the injustice go on too long.

I stood at the window, tears running down my face, the heat of the flames warming the room. "Why?" shouted its way through my head like a wayward drummer gone berserk. I responded warily to the touch on my shoulder. My landlady looked at me, resignation spread like a blanket over her face. "The firemen say we have to go. The building will be tinder in no time." I took her outstretched hand and moved from the safety of my room to the world where sanity no longer reigned.

She and I wandered through the streets that night, helping to calm people, bandaging up wounds from fights and police sticks. In the morning, a surreal world greeted me. Charred timbers held nothing but smoke, wafting into the bright sunshine. People huddled in groups, sobs enveloped the air. Dogs scavenged, chewing on the bodies of fried birds and squirrels.

Yet nothing was different. Headlines in the paper proclaimed the damage was in the millions and was done by the residents of the area. Next to it, a story of several GIs—all black—dead that morning in Vietnam.

The following months showed the escalating of the war in Vietnam and the escalating of the war for equal rights for black Americans. The anger, the confusion, the unrest in this nation was palpable. Fire continued to destroy neighborhoods across the country. The fire consumed whatever was in its path, demonstrating the anger that filled the hearts of marginalized people.

In November, the anger reached a peak, as more and more young men of all races returned home in coffins decorated with American flags. I joined some people from my neighborhood and boarded a bus to Washington, D.C. The march planned was a protest against the war and the senseless killing.

The bus pulled into the mall area a little before the sunset that day. People milled all around, bundled up against the cold and against the angry barbs that came from those who supported the war. I took in the faces— young, old, rich, poor, tear-streaked, stoic. I watched as empty wooden coffins were brought before the Capitol, representing young men killed in the war.

Dark descended and the wind died down. With the body warmth of thousands, the night didn't seem so cold. I talked to my neighbor about the day's news, about the ride down, and suddenly a chill swept through me. The light was there again—the light that had streamed through my window months ago. But I wasn't in my room. I was here, outside the Capitol with thousands of people, but I could feel the fire.

I turned, expecting the same scene of growing devastation. Instead, I saw one wool-hat-crowned, middle-aged woman lighting the candle of the long-haired hippie next to her. He in turn lit the candle of a distinguished-looking black woman, who in turn lit the candle of the young boy next to her. I watched as that flame was passed from person to person. As each candle was lit, the features of the person receiving the light stood out, the fire giving each a chance to be highlighted in a unique way.

Gradually the fire spread, growing until the light and warmth was as strong as that evening many months ago. This fire, however, dispelled the darkness, calmed the anger, united each person. The individual flame brought hope each of us could bring to fruition. The fire was the fire of the Spirit, the confirmation that our passion would make a difference in the world, a difference not for destruction but for building together.

I grinned. In the distance someone was singing, "God is alive, magic is afoot." I knew what they were talking about.

For the Love of Darkness

Michelle Langenberg

I take great comfort in the night
when the presence of one light
appears to shine more brightly than
the summer sun on the long white sand
of some warm coastline, with the glint
of waves of sparkling breakers bent
toward laughing children on the beach.
That single light! It seems to reach
out rays from one, to one, to link
us solitary souls. I think
there is no dark or cruel damp
that can't be overcome by lamp
and love—the love of darkness, which
defines the worth of flaming wick.

Meditation: Candle Colors and What They Mean

Maril Crabtree

*W*hen meditating with candles as a source of life energy and as a symbol for the powerful qualities of fire, candle colors take on added significance.

You may want to choose a color that corresponds to one of the chakras (energy centers) of the body. If you are meditating on relationship issues, for example, you might select a green candle for the fourth, or heart, chakra.

A basic resource book on chakra functions is *Wheels of Life: A User's Guide to the Chakra System* by Judith Anodea. Choose red for the first chakra, orange for the second, yellow for the third, green for the fourth, sky blue for the fifth, dark blue (indigo) for the sixth, and white or gold for the seventh. White candles can also encompass the entire color spectrum.

Consider the symbolic meanings of the colors, which are sometimes broader than the chakra colors. Red is the symbol for vibrant health and energy. As the basic color of fire, it also relates to sexuality and fertility. Orange is also a color for attracting and deepening sexual energy. Yellow can be used for mental clarity and also, especially in its deeper gold shades, for prosperity.

Green is for growth and renewal, relationship and connection, and financial abundance. Purple and blue are both spiritual colors used to promote healing and to create an environment of serenity and peace. Both white and black can be used for purity, and black can be used to absorb negative energies. One of the best sources to consult for more detailed symbolic meanings of candle colors and how to use them is *Sticks, Stones, Roots & Bones* by Stephanie Rose Bird.

In addition to applying these universal meanings, it's important to stay open to any intuitive guidance that comes to you about the significance of a color and its application to your life situation at that moment.

Finally, keep in mind that the candle flame itself encompasses a spectrum of colors: red, orange, yellow, blue, green, white, and all shades in between. The energy of fire is in your DNA, in your cells, and in that part of consciousness that partakes of collective memory.

When you light a candle, you invite the powerful protection, rituals, and energy of that flame that has existed from generation to generation and from culture to culture, throughout the ages.

Contributors

Laurie Adams lives in McKean, Pennsylvania, with her soul mate and husband of thirty years. They have two living children, Tom and Tina, and two adorable grandchildren, Alanis and Carter. Contact her at Hherstory99@aol.com.

Leslie Howard Antley is a perpetual student of the universe, as well as the local university. She has varied interests, including anthropology, archaeology, linguistics, genealogy, history, religion, and philosophy. She also enjoys attempting to solve the puzzles of life. When not actively chasing flutter-bys, she spends meditation time creating memories with her hands through crocheting, embroidering, and crazy quilting. A fifth generation native Texan, she lives in Houston with her husband, Mark, and feline companions, Ruby and Pippin.

Barbara Ardinger, Ph.D., is the author of *Finding New Goddesses* and *Quicksilver Moon,* as well as *Goddess Meditations* and *Practicing the Presence of the Goddess.* Her day job is freelance editing for people who don't want to embarrass themselves in print. She works with authors of nonfiction books on spiritual, metaphysical, and other topics, and she also edits novels. She lives in southern California. Contact her through her Web site at *www. barbaraardinger.com.*

Kristine Babe has been thrilled with the written word since she fell for her first favorite story, *I Love Grandma*. It didn't take her long to turn in her crayons for pens; she's been writing ever since. Kristine has written corporate communications, marketing materials, poetry, and personal essays. She is now writing short fiction and plans to write a novel. Kristine lives in southeastern Wisconsin with her husband and two children. Contact her at kbabe@wi.rr.com.

Stephanie Rose Hunt Bird is author of *Four Seasons of Mojo: Sticks, Stones, Roots and Bones: Hoodoo, Mojo and Conjuring with Herbs; A Walkabout Home;* and *Motherland Herbal*. Her prose is featured in the magazines *Age Ain't Nothin' But a Number: Black Women Explore Mid-Life*; and *Natural Home, Herb Quarterly*, and *Sage Woman*. She taught painting at the School of the Art Institute of Chicago and is a hereditary intuitive and visionary specializing in African healing wisdom. Contact her at BirdoSan@aol.com.

Julie Biro says she is "an ordinary person living an extraordinary life." She explains that "it is lived within me and reflected back to me through my daily interaction with the bush, its creatures, my companion animals, my husband, and the elemental forces that shape all our lives. In the moments of grace when I detach and become the silent witness, I can connect with all life and know her true nature."

Rob Bosanko lives in Arkansas, where he taught drama for nearly thirty years. He graduated from Emporia State University. He considers this publication a return to his roots. His wife also teaches drama. They have two children, Jamie and Addie. Rob has written many plays, which have been produced at Emporia State, the New Stage in Jackson, and the South Arkansas Arts Center. He is presently finishing his first novel. Contact him at jewarnock8@cox-internet.com.

Jennifer Brown is a writer and stay-at-home mother of three. Her writing credits include honorable mention fiction and poetry in *Writer's Journal* and *Byline*, as well as an award of first place in Liberty, Missouri's 2004 Poetry and Prominent People competition. Publishing credits include fiction, nonfiction, and poetry in *Long Story Short*, *The Storyteller*, and *The Liberty Tribune*.

Anna Buckner still feels like a phoenix. She is a freelance writer who lives with her husband, Bob, and two big dogs, Buffy-the-squirrel-slayer and Hercule-the-muttweiler. She hopes she is aware enough now to prevent any more drastic wake-up calls from Above. So far, so good.

Candace Carrabus likes to play with fire; that's why she writes. Her award-winning stories have appeared in the journals *The St. Louis Suburban Journals*, *The Storyteller*, and *The Rockford Review*, as well as in *A Cup of Comfort for Courage*. She keeps three horses on the farm she shares with her architect husband, one delightful daughter, numerous cats, and a large black lab named Alex. Contact her through her Web site at *www. CandaceCarrabus.com*.

Dane Cervine lives in Santa Cruz, California, where he serves as Chief of Children's Mental Health for the county. His work has recently appeared in journals such as *Eclipse, Freshwater, Raven Chronicles*, and *Porter-Gulch Review*. His work has also appeared in recent anthologies: *To Love One Another: Poems Celebrating Marriage ; Working Hard for the Money: America's Working Poor in Poem & Story; Pagan's Muse;* and *My Heart's First* Steps. Contact him at *danecervine@cruzio.com*.

Dru Clarke, a former marine science and ecology teacher, does natural history writing and helps her husband care for a small ranch in the Flint Hills of Kansas, where they raise quarter horses. She also facilitates Leopold Education Project workshops, which focus on developing a sense of place and a strong land ethic. Contact her at *druc@kansas.net*.

Ann Clizer lives in the mountains northeast of Sandpoint, Idaho. Her work has appeared in regional and national publications. She is writing a collection of stories about life in the backwoods, titled *On Higher Ground*. Ann strives to capture the unique blend of commonplace and bizarre that makes up the human experience. She operates a construction business with her husband, but her heart is on the water in a blue kayak. Contact her at *annclizer@sisna.com*.

Rev. Karen Coussens delights in her gift for storytelling, discovered as the mother of six and enhanced as the grandmother of nineteen and great-grandmother of two. Now living in a yurt on eighty acres in Northwest Michigan, Karen is learning new stories daily—stories of joy and peace in connecting with nature. She may be contacted at *kaycee@coslink.net*.

Angelique Cuillierier is a nomme-de-feu of a recluse who lives in a distant land. She has been writing articles, book reviews, children's stories, and plays under various names for many years. You may reach her by contacting the author of this book.

Deborah Davis writes fiction for young people, teaches writing workshops, and escapes to the wilderness as often as possible. Her novels are *The Secret of the Seal* and *My Brother Has AIDS*, and she is the editor of *You Look Too Young to Be a Mom: Teen Mothers Speak Out on Love, Learning, and Success*. She lives in Berkeley with her husband and son. Contact her through her Web site at *www.teenmombook.com*.

Frances Derhy, born in London, has lived for the past thirty years in a communal village in the foothills of Jerusalem, Israel. Working as a preschool teacher gave her the opportunity to spend many happy hours checking out wildflowers, birds, and bugs in the surrounding pine forest. Frances writes stories for children and has been known to draw and dabble in other handicrafts. She is the mother of six and grandmother of five. Contact her at Derhy_@neve-ilan.co.il.

Peggy Eastman is the award-winning author of *Godly Glimpses: Discoveries of the Love That Heals*, and editor of *Share*, a spiritual quarterly published by the Catholic Daughters of the Americas. Her work has appeared in many national publications including *Guideposts*, *Ladies Home Journal*, *SELF*, *Working Mother*, and *AARP Bulletin*. Contact her at peggyeastman@cs.com or *www.bookviews.com/ BookPage/godlyglimpses.html*.

Karl Elder, author of five collections of poetry, including *Phobophobia*, *A Man in Pieces*, and *The Geocryptogrammatist's Pocket Compendium of the United States*, is Lakeland College's Fessler Professor of Creative Writing and Poet in Residence. Among honors are a Pushcart Prize, the Lucien Stryk Award, grants from the Illinois Arts Council for poetry and fiction, and Lakeland's Outstanding Teacher Award. For over two decades Elder has edited *Seems;* contact him through the magazine's Web site: *http://www1.lakeland.edu/seems*.

Jean M. Farber was born in Milwaukee, Wisconsin, and grew up in the Midwest. After graduating from the University of Illinois, she lived in Paris for a year and Morocco for three years as a Peace Corps volunteer. Her first career was in publishing. Later she received a master's degree in teaching. She has taught French, Spanish, and English as a Second Language for eight years. She currently teaches Spanish in Steilacoom, Washington. Contact her at jeanmichalski@msn.com.

Charles Adés Fishman is director of the Distinguished Speakers Program at Farmingdale State University, associate editor of *The Drunken Boat*, and poetry editor of *New Works Review*. His books include *Mortal Companions*, *The Firewalkers*, and *The Death Mazurka*, nominated for the 1990 Pulitzer Prize in

Poetry. His fifth book, *Country of Memory* , as well as his tenth chapbook, *5,000 Bells*, were published in 2004.

Maureen Tolman Flannery's latest book is *Ancestors in the Landscape: Poems of a Rancher's Daughter.* Other books are *Secret of the Rising Up: Poems of Mexico; Knowing Stones: Poems of Exotic Places*; and *Remembered into Life*. Maureen grew up on a Wyoming sheep ranch, but she and her actor husband, Dan, raised four children in Chicago. Her work has appeared in numerous anthologies and literary journals including *Midwest Quarterly Review, Amherst Review, Slant, Buckle&*, and *Atlanta Review*. Contact her at mtflannery@earthlink. net.

Grace Flora is a member of Art Culture Nature and of Interhelp. She is a native plant advocate with a special interest in the interface between poetry and biology.

Virginia Fortner is an educational consultant, a teacher for homebound programs, adjunct professor of special education at several metropolitan colleges, and a guide for Footprints, a study-travel experience. She does watercolors. Most of her published work has been informational in nature, but writing poetry and fiction brings her true joy.

Barbara C. Frohoff was born in St. Louis, Missouri, and has an M. A. in creative writing. She spent most of her working life in social work, and she now travels extensively in other countries. She and her husband have six children and six grandchildren. She writes fiction, travel articles, and poetry.

B. A. Goodjohn, originally from the UK, now resides in Forest, Virginia. Her poetry and short stories have appeared in *The Texas Review*, *The Cortland Review*, *Blue Cubicle Press*, *Flashquake*, and other journals. Contact her at bunny@worshipthecarrot.com.

Susan Elizabeth Hale is a singer, poet, and music therapist. She is author of *Song and Silence: Voicing the Soul* (1995) and the forthcoming *Sacred Space—Sacred Sound*. Susan teaches workshops and classes throughout the United States, Great Britain, and Canada and directs The Voice of the Rose: Songkeeper Apprenticeship Program in Taos, New Mexico. For more information, visit *www. angelfire.com/nm/susong* or e-mail susong@yahoo.com.

Carolyn Hall is a freelance writer. Her works appear in *Sacred Stones* and *Chicken Soup to Inspire a Woman's Soul*. She is marketing director for *Kansas City Voices* and serves on the board of Whispering Prairie Press.

Patricia Hamill divides her time between the rural New Jersey cottage she shares with her husband, a professional potter, and her family's home in upstate New York. She spends her days writing essays and children's fiction, and running her business, Heron Moon Editorial Services. In her precious spare hours, she rides her horse, Latin Quarter, hides away weaving peacefully on her loom, or devours works of Irish literature. Contact her at thamill@hotmail.com.

Jessica Hankinson has published in magazines such as *The Growing Edge*, *Weatherwise*, and *The World & I*. She earned a B.A. in biology from Ohio Wesleyan

University, an M.S. in botany from the University of Wisconsin–Madison, and an M.A. in English from Clemson University. Her career as educator began with teaching English at Clemson University; currently she teaches science at TL Hanna High School. Jessica and husband, Brian, live in Pendleton, South Carolina. Contact her at jhankinson@earthlink.net.

Sherry Norman Horbatenko lives in Southeast Georgia, in a small town of milk and honey called Woodbine. She shares her life with two paperweights (who greatly resemble cats) and her mother. She tutors and maintains a small farm, a home business, and two rental properties. She has written short stories and a fantasy novel with two sequels in process. She's looking for a good agent who will take her work and help to make "it" happen. Contact her at horbaten@gate.net.

Mary Ann Horn resides on the banks of Julington Creek in North Florida. She has taught religious studies at Flagler College and women's studies in the Honors Program at the University of North Florida. She holds a graduate degree from the University of Our Lady (Notre Dame). Her written work has appeared in *Water's Edge* magazine. Contact her at maryronhorn@comcast.net.

Greg Eric Hultman is a writer living and working in Chicago. Starting his writing career as a news reporter, he also wrote for state natural resource agencies and later worked as a copywriter. He majored in creative writing and graduated from John Schultz's Story Workshop program. A professional interpretive naturalist at the Shedd Aquarium, Hultman is author of a book on botany in the Midwest, numerous magazine articles, book contributions, and several media scripts. Contact him at sagedancer@sbcglobal.net.

Roberta Beach Jacobson is an American freelance writer living in Greece. Her publishing credits include *Woman's Day, McCall's, Capper's, Playgirl,* and *I Love Cats* magazines, and her work appears in seventeen anthologies. Contact her at *www.travelwriters.com/ Roberta.*

nwenna kai is a writer, TV/Film producer, and restaurateur. She co-owns a live foods vegan cafe in West Hollywood, California, called Taste of the Goddess Cafe. Overall, she loves art, yoga, organic live food, good people, good music, sun bathing, and holistic spas. She resides in Los Angeles.

Kathleen Kirk is an editor of *RHINO Magazine,* a literary annual (*www.rhinopoetry.org*). Her poetry and prose appear in many journals, including *ACM, Midnight Mind, Poetry East, Puerto del Sol, Quarter After Eight,* and *Willow Review.* Kathleen and her husband, painter Tony Rio, are parents of two children.

Joan Koerper, Ph.D., received her doctorate in humanities from the California Institute of Integral Studies, San Francisco, California, and delighted in writing her dissertation, *Singing Over the Bones: Pottery and Writing as Expressions of Soul as Artist, A Work of Creative Nonfiction.* She is a writer, potter, adjunct professor, workshop leader, licensed psychotherapist, and former detective. She lives in California. Contact her at Koerper@aol.com.

Michelle Langenberg is a poet, artist, freelance editor, and energy healer. Langenberg has won awards from the World Order of Narrative and Formalist Poets and the Scottish Open Poetry Competition. Credits include more than 100 works of art, poetry, prose, and songs published in *Sparrow*, *The Formalist*, *Southern Humanities Review*, *Black Bear Review*, and *Exposure Art*, among others. Contact her at chelleashes@kc.rr.com.

Claire MacDonell grew up in rural Nova Scotia where winter still means something. She's been a social worker for a number of years, but is presently a south-bound traveler, learning Spanish and working in gardens along the way. Her biggest goal is to get all the way to the bottom of Argentina. Contact her at Clairemacdonell@hotmail.com.

Hualani Janice Mark is a muse maven, a transformational performer and musician, a mother, fertility liaison, visionary writer, and world traveler offering womb wisdom workshops, dedicating her services to the fulfillment of our human destiny. As a visioneering businesswoman and regeneration strategist, she's establishing a new reality for communication and leadership wisdom through SOULsignatures and her unique enterprising program called BLISSbiz. Contact her through the Web sites *www.museonthemove.com*, *www.design-oracle.com*, or *www.paradiseposse.com*.

Ian McDonald has lived in Guyana since 1955. He is author of the novel *The Hummingbird Tree* and several books of poems. He is editor of the journal *Kyk-Over-Al* and joint editor of the *Heinemann Book of Caribbean Poetry*, as well as a Fellow of the Royal Society of Literature.

Diane Queen Miller lives in northwest Montana, follows the traditional ways of the Lakota Nation, and works with the Ikeya Wicasa (The Common People) Native American Cultural Center. She also works as a radio copywriter/producer, loves native beading and leatherwork, and dances in local powwows. Her life goals are to be a grandma who bakes cookies and tells stories, and to have her voice on audio books for children and adults.

Suruchi Mohan lives in California. Since writing this story, her first novel has been accepted by an agent. She is now working on a new novel.

Patricia Monaghan is the author of numerous books on spirituality including *The Red-Haired Girl from the Bog: The Landscape of Celtic Myth and Spirit*, as well as three books of poetry, most recently *Dancing with Chaos*. She is on the interdisciplinary faculty of DePaul University in Chicago. Her Web site is *www.patriciamonaghanpoetry.com*.

Rafe Montello has been attracted to mysticism and personal development all his life. His studies have included mind-body arts ranging from aikido, baquazhang, Brazilian jujitsu, and kali escrima, to yoga and pilates. A Buddhist for over thirty years, he explores practices from many traditions. His formal education includes a graduate degree in educational psychology and training as a chef. Information on his program using cooking in personal development can be found at *www.werecookingnow.org*.

Tammy Murray lives in Pawtucket, Rhode Island, and works as an activities director at an independent retirement community. Her husband Tim works as an executive chef. Now that her children are grown, she spends free time working toward a college degree, learning to play piano, gardening, and crocheting. Tammy recently moved to a new home in Pawtucket. She looks forward to many cozy evenings in front of her new fireplace. Contact her at writermom960@yahoo.com.

J. Eva Nagel is cofounder of Side By Side, a Youth Leadership Program, and the founder of the Waldorf School of Saratoga Springs, New York. She maintains a private psychotherapy practice in Schenectady, and she is a staff development consultant, an essayist, an avid traveler, and an overextended gardener. Most importantly, she is mother of four and grandmother of two. Contact her at jevan424@aol.com.

James Penha, a native New Yorker, teaches at the Jakarta International School in Indonesia. Among recent published works are an article in NCTE's *ClassroomNotes Plus*, a story in *Columbia*, and poems in *Heliotrope*, *Thema*, and *PoetryMagazine.com*. A volume of his *Greatest Hits* is available from Pudding House as part of its series celebrating the work of small-press poets. Contact him at jpenha@cbn.net.id.

Jan Phillips is a speaker and workshop director who teaches throughout the U.S. She is the author of *Marry Your Muse, God Is at Eye Level:Photography as a Healing Art,* and *Divining the Body: A Journey Through the Sacred Self.* To receive her free online Museletter, email jan@janphillips.com.

Art Ritas taught English for thirty-three years. He led interdisciplinary study tours to the Yucatan in Mexico and was codirector of the Center for Teaching and Learning at Macomb Community College. Now in Naples, Florida, with his wife, Susan, an anthropologist, he is a boat captain, master naturalist, and facilitator of creative writing workshops. He is writing a book on his kayak adventures on the Wilderness Waterway in Everglades National Park. Contact him at Aritas540@aol.com.

Penny Ross is a writer and artist living in Northern Virginia. She works in television part-time, which gives her ample opportunity to write, paint, and sculpt. Penny has been showing her watercolors and photography for many years, and she has recently embarked on writing for publication. View her other works at *www.penzart.com*.

Joy Margaret Sallans lives in Ottawa, Canada, with her husband, John, their cat and two parrots. Her work as a lay pastoral visitor with the Unitarian Church, as well as her studies in palliative care, have taught her the need for spiritual self-nurturing. Joy takes every opportunity to walk the labyrinth, lit or otherwise. An active member of Ottawa's crime-writing community, she writes about the mysterious and supernatural and is a founding member of CrimeStarters (*www.crimestarters.com*).

Julie Ann Shapiro is a freelance writer. Her short stories and essays have appeared in *Mega Era, Millennium Shift, Orgease Journal, Alternate Species, Story South, Science Fiction and Fantasy World, Seven Seas Magazine, Word Riot, The Write Line, Green Tricycle, All Things Girl, Ultimate Hallucination, The Glut, Somewhat, Dovetail Journal, Uber, Moon Dance, The Quarterly Staple,* and *Opium.* Julie is working on her second novel. Contact her at Julie@gotdot.com.

Carol Shenold is a nationally published freelance writer with articles appearing in medical professional and general interest magazines. Writing is an important part of her life, helping keep her sane, along with playing dulcimer music and portrait painting. As she gets older, she finds herself trying to pay attention to more of those little things so important in life, such as children and sunsets, as well as learning to accept miracles when they happen. Contact her at cshenold@cox.net.

Shumalua is mother of three and grandmother of nine children, and encourages all people to wear red on Friday to express compassion and concern for the bloodshed of innocent people everywhere and the plight of our environment. "May we find each other in the silence between the words."

Roberta Gordon Silver (aka R. Gordon Silver) is a novelist whose books are sold online at *www.authorhouse. com* or *www.booksamillion.com*. *Power Within*, a romantic suspense tale of New Age zeal gone wrong imperils the heroine, who saves herself by her wits and inner strength. *Voices of Eternity* is an inspirational historical novel based on anecdotes by her immigrant father. Contact her at silverbob765@yahoo.com.

Diane Sims lives in Stratford, Ontario, Canada. Her books include *Gardens of Our Souls* (in English, Chinese, and Japanese), *An Ovarian Cancer Companion* (in English and French), and *Solace,* as well as various anthology submissions. She is accompanied in her life's walk by both multiple sclerosis and ovarian cancer. Diane adopted three feral kittens who give her many smiles, along with the love of her life, Garth, who has reappeared to be by her side. Contact her at dianesims@rogers.com.

Michael Sky has facilitated firewalks for more than 5,000 people since 1984. He is author of *Dancing with the Fire*, a comprehensive exploration of the scientific, psychological, and spiritual teachings of fire (*www. dancingwiththefire.com*) and *Breathing*, a definitive book on the use of breath for therapeutic and spiritual benefits (*www.energybreath.com*). Michael lives with his wife and daughter on a small green island in the Pacific Northwest. Contact him at sky@thinkingpeace.com.

Richard Smyth has published poems in such journals as *The Southern Poetry Review, The Florida Review, Tampa Review, Kansas Quarterly*, and others. He is editor and publisher of the poetry journal *Albatross*, now in its twentieth year. He holds a Ph.D. in English from the University of Florida and currently lives in Haverhill, Massachusetts.

Bernadette Stankard describes herself as "a flower child gone to seed." She has been married for thirty-three years to Ed, who was at the Washington protest at the same time as she, unbeknown to each of them. Their two children follow in their parents' footsteps by protesting and working for change. Bernadette has authored several short stories and nonfiction pieces. Her most recent book is *How Each Child Learns: Using Multiple Intelligences in Faith Formation*. Contact her at stankard@sbcglobal. net.

Ola Szeleczky, born in Ukraine, now lives in Australia. Being a fire element, she is deeply inspired by nature's ability to regenerate itself after bush fires. She follows the spiritual teachings of Mata Amritanandamayi (Amma), has worked as a crisis counselor, and writes poetry.

Sharon Upp, of Laguna Niguel, California, has been a writer for more than twenty years, working as National Coordinator of English for *Voluntad Editorial* in Bogota, Colombia, editor of trade journals in the States, author of an Orange County business journal astrology column, and author of poetry and vignettes. She taught A Course in Miracles, served with the Alliance for Spiritual Community, and is an ordained minister of the Living Essence Foundation. Contact her at sjmilesupp@cox. net.

Amethyst Wyldfyre (Maryjane Moore) is a spiritual counselor and healer living in the Merrimack Valley of Southern New Hampshire. She is also a talented jewelry designer, artist, and writer. She is owner of Amethyst Wyldfyre, A Sanctuary for Awakening to the Sacred, a home for her work and the work of other artist/healers who specialize in creating sacred objects. Contact her at stonemedicine@comcast.net.

Andy Young is an artist/teacher of creative writing at NOCCA/Riverfront in New Orleans. Her most recent book is *All Fires the Fire*, and her chapbook, *mine*, was recently reprinted. Her poems have recently appeared in Dublin's *The Stinging Fly*, *Carolina Quarterly*, and the anthology *Another South*. Her words have been featured in electronic music, dance, and theater productions, and have been translated into four languages. Contact her at andimuse@att.net.

Other Titles Available:

Inspirational writings exploring the sacred human connection to nature.

Sacred Stones

1-59337-113-6
$10.95 ($15.95 CAN)

Sacred Feathers

1-58062-707-2
$10.95 ($17.95 CAN)

Sacred Waters

1-59337-286-8
$10.95 ($14.95 CAN)

Available wherever books are sold.
Or call 1-800-258-0929, or visit us at *www.adamsmedia.com*

one ad to come